SINGING into BONE

SINGING into BONE

STORIES of VISION and HEALING

by Rebecca Singer

ISBN 978-1-64007-560-3

Printed in the United States of America

www.shamanicenergy.com

BABA YAGA
PRESS

This book is dedicated to my first teacher, Patricia Spradling, who taught me how to take a leap of faith and enter fully into The Great Mystery and to Marsha Graham, who showed me how to land on my own two feet.

I would like to thank Cait Johnson for her wonderful, detailed work editing this book, and her unwavering belief in it. Also, a thank you to Reid Hannan for his design work and to Baba Yaga Publishing.

A thank you to Shannon Kiningham for helping me remember details about Patricia. And Elizabeth Cunningham for her encouragement, as well as my husband, William Eadie for his support in the writing of this book.

CONTENTS

III. LIVING WITH THE REINDEER PEOPLE

IV. SINGING into BONE

FOREWORD

Reading *Singing into Bone* is like walking a labyrinth. The tales Rebecca Singer weaves together are not linear; they spiral and turn, they take us to the edge of the unknown, then circle back home, deeper than before. Like the windings of the labyrinth, the stories have a heartbeat, a pulse.

There are four sections in the book, just as there are four directions and four gates in a Medicine Wheel. The book opens with a powerful prayer. The stories reveal answers that have come to Rebecca throughout her courageous, compassionate and adventurous life.

Rebecca Singer is a vivid and generous writer, inviting us with her into the home of her beloved first teacher, Patricia, sharing her eccentric humor and wisdom. She takes us with her as she walks in the Costa Rican rainforest at night or faces charging reindeer in Mongolia. She shares with us her remarkable ability to enter into sympathetic relationship with all life forms, small an inchworm, huge as a raging wind. She shows us what healing looks like through the eyes of a born, and extensively trained, healer.

Dear fellow readers, you can trust this storyteller, her humor, her humility, her honesty. Keep your skepticism, as Patricia always encouraged Rebecca to do. But do allow yourself the joy of entering fully into these wonder tales. I believe that as you absorb these stories something in you will ease and open, and you will know, as Rebecca expresses it, that you are "held in the lap of Mother Earth."

– Elizabeth Cunningham
author of *The Maeve Chronicles*

INTRODUCTION

A Prayer

I call on the great wisdom of the earth to guide and protect me.

To take me as I am and nurture me, my belly flat against your desert.

To open the roots of strength, half hidden, but knowable.

To show me my allies and guide me.

I humbly offer my open heart, knowledge of infinite goodness,

eternal tenderness and magical creation from energy to form.

I accept my path with its obstacles and challenges. I see my reflection

in the clear desert lake as a healer, changer, and hope I may reach those waters.

And when the ground beneath my feet is crumbling, and I am falling and

lost in fear, I will hold to the wisdom of the gentle breezes…look to the light

that is the hand of grace, ready to ease my heartache and heal my fall.

Let the earth be our Mother and let our true natures be free.

This prayer came out of my mouth as I lay flat on the Eastern Oregon desert sand. Where did it come from? I wrote the words down afterward, because I knew even then that they showed me a path—a path toward a future that was unknown to me at the time. And yet it seemed that, somewhere deep inside me, that path was clear.

Rereading it now, years later, I am struck by how our prayers are answered. People say to be careful what you ask for. I would say…. we can't possibly know the form or timing of how our prayers will be answered. But they are.

It has taken over 30 years of my life to step fully into the realm of the Healer Shaman. For many years, my prayer has been to align being of service with the timing of the universe, and to trust in that timing and alignment. When my first teacher, Patricia, and I decided that my next teacher would be the rainforest of Costa Rica, I waited till my son told me it was OK to go there….and then I left. I only knew that I had a place to stay, in exchange for doing healing work on someone twice a month. I didn't know the language and I only had a little money. But I went because it was my path. In the same way, when it became clear to me that I was called back to the States, I ripped myself apart from that land, although it was so painful that I thought I would die in the process. Still, I placed my trust in my inner knowing. And it has led me to the place I am now. It is a good place.

I always begin classes by saying "I am neither Lakota nor Siberian. So we are already one important step away from the source. I have permission to teach you from my teachers. The fact that I have given you reading materials means we are two steps away, as traditionally all this knowledge was handed down through stories. And perhaps, most importantly, everything I am going to teach really cannot be taught intellectually; it is, in the end, absorbed through a way of life that we are much distanced from. All that being said, I do think there is great value in the teachings as long as you understand we are many steps away from the truth of those who live these teachings on a day to day basis."

I was given permission by my teachers to teach, offer Ceremonies, classes, healings, and workshops. But in my over thirty years of practice, when all is said and done, my greatest teacher has been and always will be nature.

I had no idea when I spoke my prayer that it would be answered. Who knew that my path would take me to many states in the US, to Canada, Trinidad, Costa Rica, Mongolia? Who knew? Today I look into the desert lake waters and see a self reflected who has lived and is living that prayer.

This life has not been easy, but then I did not ask for easy. I asked for real. I have had to be very aware of my own "stuff" in order to separate personal from not-personal, and I have had to stay in very good physical condition to have the energy to teach and work in the way I do. This requires time and effort—more, as I age. This life requires a level of self care. I have not wanted to end up as other shamans I've known who became ill from their work. The work also requires a mental strength that is challenging to me, as I cannot let myself get lost in dark thoughts. I cannot let anxiety, fear, or grief overwhelm me in my personal life, as it affects the healing work. So I have had to learn to sit with these feelings and let them pass.

I also have to go outdoors and give my energy out to the universe, otherwise it collects in my body in mysterious ways: painful lumps on my head, or swellings or pain here or there that the medical world cannot understand. Fortunately I live in an area peopled with grounded, talented alternative healers who help me when I need assistance.

While I go about my little life, and try to, bit by bit, to close the gap between my daily being and my Spirit, I know that it takes an Earth Walk to bring these two into harmony. Once the drama of being a human becomes familiar, and if a person is blessed to live enough years to see enough cycles of drama to step out of them, there is actually an opening for grace.

For me, grace is having the time to notice sunlight on a drop of water in the forest. To listen to the inner yearning for a grandchild and at the same time remind myself there is nothing to be done about it, as it's not my business.

When the kitty litter box is cleaned, the prayers said, the dishes washed, the altar honored, it's this day to day existence that we have.

The older I get, the more important kindness becomes, yet in the face of the desecration of the earth, and so many socio-political attitudes I simply cannot abide, it becomes more and more challenging for me to maintain it. I have often felt like a creature dropped onto a planet during a time that was not of my liking, though I do believe I chose this time, my family, and this life form.

How to be a human being takes a lifetime to learn. I think we romanticize indigenous people because they embody a world view of wholeness. Earth-centered, earth-honoring people have the basic humility to see themselves as part of the great web of life, not a life form superior to all other beings. Perhaps we idealize other cultures and tribal life by projecting what we know to be true but no longer have ways to express.

I often wonder why, when we will be on this planet for only a nanosecond, we still persist in destruction of one another and other species, why we still dishonor native peoples and fight over land, material goods, whatever. We fight and fight till there may be nothing left to fight for.

The many times I have held newborns in my arms, I don't see fighters, destroyers, or creatures who feel themselves to be the owners of the earth, so I think these qualities must be learned. Perhaps we contain all possibilities as humans, and our families, cultures, the times we live in, the place on earth we are born to—all these contribute to the parts of us that come forth, the ways we show up in the world.

My intention in writing this book is to introduce you to the beauty of the shaman's path, and to offer the wisdom and lessons I've learned over the years in the form of stories. It is my prayer that we will walk our lives with respect for all beings. May these stories help you find your way, as they have helped me find mine.

PART I

A SHAMAN'S ROOTS

WATERFALL

It's happening again. I'm in my twenties, sitting behind a waterfall, my body permeated with sound, with multilayered harmonies, as if every being that has lived, lives, or will live on this planet is making a clear flute-like tone to the heavens. The sound is all-encompassing; I am lost in it, the passing of time, the damp droplets from the rushing water that spray me.

My eyes closed, I'm crying; I am melting into sound. I feel myself starting to be pulled upward, as if leaving my body, but the sensation alarms me, and I open my eyes.

No, I have not taken any drugs or plant medicine, I am simply experiencing one of the many openings into another realm of being that have occurred unpredictably since I was a child. I had no idea as I was walking through the Northern California forest that slowly my vision would shift, everything would brighten, and the sight of individual lichen growing amid mossy green logs would bring me to tears.

All I can think is, "It's happening," this opening in the air around me, a shift like a slight wavering of light that precedes these altered states of being. I did not plan to notice the waterfall in the distance, or to be drawn to it with the strong pull of the moon on the tides. I didn't know I would discover the fern-shielded entryway so I could sit behind the waterfall. It's with a shock that the chorus of beings overwhelms my senses. In fact, I jump away, afraid. But then, as always, my curiosity gets the better of me, and I reenter this watery sanctum to listen.

There is no room for thought. The sound is literally vibrating the air around me, and as I open my eyes, I can see each individual water drop falling, in slow motion, each droplet that was a part of the cascading waterfall. A voice through the chorus tells me, "You are always somewhere. " I do not try to make sense of this; it's like a whisper on water.

When I can't take any more, I roll out onto the ground, crying, wet, and overwhelmed with the beauty of that sound, which has stayed with me my whole life.

When I returned to my little cottage in Berkeley, a friend called to ask how my walk had been, and I realized I had no language to express the experience and no one in my life who could understand what had happened to me. This was the crux of the issue: this sense of aloneness with the many experiences that opened to me without my control, at totally unexpected moments, and that seemed to catapult me into another realm.

Although it was a beautiful experience, it left me drained and lonely. I so yearned to find someone who could make sense of these openings. In fact, I had visions of one day purchasing desert land, far away from anyone, and simply going there to ask for a teacher. Somehow I thought the clarity of the desert would make my voice heard. I did not know, on that day, when I met the spirits of All Who Have Come, that I would indeed be lying on the bare desert earth a few years later begging for someone who understood.

TRAIN RIDE

I am captivated by old women I can see out of my train window, bent over in fields of what was then Yugoslavia. My head pressed to the window, I see they wear tattered skirts and shawls, heads covered for protection from the sun. The cold window on my face is a relief from the overheated train, and as I watch, I see that the women appear to be working with hay bales, as well as picking something I cannot see.

They look like paintings by an unknown artist, representations of an ancient crow-like culture, the fields they labor in not plentiful, but covered in some sorrowful attempts at growth. My eyes are filled with light golds and browns, but the grey skies cast a gloom on all of it.

I am traveling through parts of Europe to assist in family therapy workshops. This particular train ride is feeling heavy and somehow dreamlike. As I watch the swiftly passing fields, a shift in my vision begins, and I see a war- torn country outside the window. I see dead, bloody bodies, and hear the sounds of war, cries and screams, the rat a tat tat of gunshots and the boom of cannons. I catch glimpses of cities being destroyed and once-friends now armed and killing each other. I see this as an overlay on the fields, as if two time frames have coalesced into one.

My stomach churns and my heartbeat quickens, as I no longer know if I am traveling through a war zone or not. One of the women turns to me as the train passes and pleads for help by holding her hands outstretched to the train. She is wounded, and trying to lift part of a bale of hay. The image is very disturbing and without being aware, I let out a cry which brings me to the present.

Fortunately no one is sitting directly beside me, but I am aware of being stared at curiously by the man across from me. I turn to him and say, "Excuse me, I was having a bad dream." He nods in understanding and goes back to reading his newspaper.

The problem is, I am not dreaming. I am wide awake, and having what I refer to as "an opening." Sometimes these shifts are openings into the past, and I hear and see what has happened in a particular place. Other times the warp is into the future. I can tell the difference by the quality of feeling. This is definitely a glimpse of the future in Yugoslavia.

As the ride continues, the air in the train feels heavier and heavier, until I am having trouble breathing. I feel closed in; the weight of the war is now in the train car and we are surrounded by death. I get up and walk quickly through several cars to get my balance and bring myself into the present.

All through Yugoslavia I have this sense of impending destruction. It's 1968, and I am certain this country is going to come apart at the seams. I see it in the women. I see it in the bales of hay that come apart on their own, won't remain in their neat and tidy forms. I hear it in the cries of the women and the gunshots and bombings and bloodshed. I see people starving, bone thin. It is a nightmare ride.

By the time I reach my destination, I am exhausted, shaken, and very puzzled. Having no control over these altered states of awareness is, even at the age of 20, beginning to weigh me down. What am I to do? Is there some responsibility that comes with such visions? Am I to ride through the countryside like Paul Revere announcing the upcoming war? What is the point of such "seeing?"

I get off the train, happy this trip is over, and wishing some wise person would greet me with an explanation of my ride.

BIRD ANGEL

My small son and I were returning from a Thanksgiving spent on my 20 acres of land in the Eastern Oregon desert. Liam was asleep in the seat beside me as I drove through the early morning dew of the desert, on the empty highway towards Mt. Hood.

My land was near a place called The Lost Forest, the only juniper and pine forest of its kind in the middle of a desert, beautiful and stark on the landscape.

I had purchased this land as a refuge, a place to wander, away from everyone. And a place to ask for help. A teacher. Each bird, insect, cloud, or lizard was an event in this landscape of sand and sage, sun and wide, expansive views. The realtor who showed me the land couldn't believe I wanted to buy it.

"Don't believe any white man has been on this land for quite awhile."

It was perfect for me, no road, just a dirt trail leading to 20 acres of desert with one tiny juniper tree for shade.

I also bought it to teach my son that life could be led simply, and I purchased a $200 mini-trailer from a man who was leaving for the National Guard. It had two small beds, a foldout table, and was perfect for sleeping and shelter. My son and I stayed in the trailer at night and made daytime excursions out to the land. We read at night by candlelight, and Liam loved it there.

On this day after Thanksgiving, having shared cold turkey sandwiches in the desert to celebrate, I was driving fast. The morning chill and light were qualities I loved, and as I drove along in my Tracker convertible, I hardly noticed the spot of black ice, as it was hidden by the shade of a tree right along the side of the road.

The car went into a spin, and I lost all sense of direction as we skidded and slid in circles on the road. I had been going at least 50mph, and as the car started to turn, Liam awoke to a world that was spinning and upside down. The car was rolling over in what felt like slow motion.

Then I saw a bird flying fast toward us from a distance. Suddenly it changed form, and became an angel with light blue wings shielding me and Liam as the car rolled a third time before crashing into the desert.

The angel told me very clearly "You and your son are going to be fine. No one is hurt. Everything is fine. It is not your time to die."

As the car lay still, I saw the angel take off, assuming once again the body of a bird.

We were upside down, and I wanted out badly. Liam had figured out which way to turn his window, and had crawled out. I did the same, and with adrenaline pumping through my system, I tried to push the car upright, rocking it back and forth. Then I grabbed Liam and held him tight. A car came along, screeched to a stop, and the next thing I remember, I was being taken in an ambulance with my neck in a brace, Liam riding up front.

When all was said and done, the car was totaled. We had rolled over three times, and people who saw the car came to the hospital when they heard what had happened. They couldn't believe that we had walked out, unharmed.

As we left the hospital, I still felt the brush of the angel's wings. Not for the first time, in fact for too many times to count, I was left with the feeling that I desperately needed someone to understand these experiences. Who else saw birds turn into angels?

In fact, part of what I was doing on that desert land, every time we visited, was asking. Asking for a teacher. I was tired of these "openings" that I could neither control nor explain. They left me feeling isolated, odd, and without a framework in which to view or appreciate them.

MEETING MY TEACHER

I had lived my whole life feeling like an emotional cripple, my heart bleeding with yearning to connect to spirit, my body tense with the aftermath of trauma. I had deep whispering voices in my heart telling me that I was whole, unbroken, untouchable in my spirit, that I just needed a different mirror in order to see and live out my true life. Those voices had kept me alive. But I felt there was a hole in my heart. Patricia was my last hope.

A friend had told me about Patricia, who referred to herself as part Irish, part Lakota. She believed that some people struggled for years with ancestral disease that had taken energetic forms in the body. This resulted in carrying on the physical, mental, or spiritual illnesses generation after generation, and her work was to stop the illness in its tracks. She performed psychic surgeries that rid the bloodline of these diseases, both backward and forward in time. I had a deep sense that this was exactly what I needed.

It was a two-hour drive to get to Patricia's house, on a road that wound up the mountain and finally became a dirt road through a gorgeous forested area near Mt. Hood. It was so strange: I found myself feeling better and better the closer I got to Patricia's address. I turned into a beautiful driveway lined with cedar and hemlock, and immediately heard the sweet sound of a creek flowing nearby.

But the English mastiff that rose, growling, to stand on the porch as I parked in the driveway was so terrifying, I could not bring myself to get out of the car. I kept waiting for someone to come to the door and take the dog inside.

I finally convinced myself that no one would leave such a huge dog outside if it was really going to attack. Gathering my courage, I stepped out of the car, and although the dog kept growling, it did step aside and allow me to ring the doorbell. I was shaking slightly, which I knew the dog could sense, but there was nothing I could do about it. I heard someone shout, "The door is open! Come on in. Leave Sheba outside, please." Since no other females were in sight, I assumed Sheba was the dog, and pushed the door open enough to slide in. Sheba continued growling.

Patricia was sitting in her workroom, and she was the size of two adults: her huge belly covered her thighs. Smoke curled from a cigarette, and she had fat little wide feet. But she had a sweet cherub face. She was coughing, and she looked pale—I found out later that she was still recovering from toxic shock. She was hardly the picture-perfect image of a healer, overweight by any standards, with heavily rouged cheeks, and the cherry-red lipstick smile of a Cheshire cat. But for the first time in my life, I felt peaceful. I had come home. I had no doubt.

"Come on in, Sweetie. You found me!"

I took in this unlikely woman sitting on the couch, too big to be able to move without great effort.

"Are you Patricia?"

"Yes ma'am, that's me. Come in. Don't just stand there. Come on in and sit here, right here, by me." Patricia indicated a place on the couch.

I looked around the room. Gigantic amethyst, huge rocks of rosey quartz. A warrior staff that guarded the room. A huge statue of the Virgin Mary. Paintings of bears. Various Native American drums. Crystals. Rattles. A buffalo hide draped over the massage table. Gorgeous colors, objects from Lakota healing traditions. The Peace Pipe in its container. The workroom.

I immediately felt at home and comfortable. And yet, looking again at Patricia, I was too surprised to speak.

"I don't bite. Honest to god, cross my heart." Patricia made a dramatic cross in the air and then burst out laughing. When Patricia laughed, she threw her head back and opened her mouth wide and her belly shook. "I may not be looking my best, but hey…this is the best it gets today!" Big laughter. "I know, I am quite a sight!"

Quite a sight, I thought. That was an understatement. My head told me that no nearly-250-pound white woman wearing a nightie with a shawl over it, smoking a cigarette and twirling her foot in the air, was any kind of teacher I wanted. But a deeper part of me knew I had met my spiritual teacher and friend.

"What are you doing? Will you please come and sit down…. you're starting to make me nervous standing over there. Come on, you made it past the guard dog. I can't be scarier than that!"

It was then I realized: all those days and months and years of feeling that my heart was leaking…. had stopped the moment I entered this room. Just like that. In a heartbeat. As if suddenly the wound had been sewn up, stitched together, the leak plugged. I was stunned by the sensation.

"Look, you have been a long time coming here. Now come and sit down. I used to be skinny too." Patricia waved me over, and patted the space on the couch again.

I sat by Patricia, feeling totally tense but also drowsy, as if I could fall asleep. I felt odd—familiar with the place. Too familiar. In fact, I felt as though this whole event had already happened. So I just sat there, unable to speak.

Meanwhile Patricia had turned on her tape recording machine, and was talking away, but I heard Patricia as if from a great distance. I was feeling profoundly disoriented, both at home and alienated. A bit, I thought, like Alice after she fell down the rabbit hole. There were just too many opposites here to be contained, and finally I blurted, "Who ARE you?"

Patricia turned off the tape recorder and was silent, staring off into space, up and to the right, while slowing twirling her bare right foot around in a clockwise direction. She began talking very softly.

"Honey, I am a teacher and a healer of sorts. People come from all over the world and find themselves here. I am very happy you are here. I think you have been on your way here for a long time, and perhaps you would like a cookie? Nothing quite like a cookie!"

Patricia offered me a plate heaped with more sugar than I had seen in one place for several years.

"No thanks, I don't eat sugar."

"Oh Lord help us all," said Patricia. "Jesus, Joseph, and Mary. You don't eat PIES?"

"Well, no…not usually." I was silent for a moment, then offered, "I eat chocolate."

"Oh thank god, hallelujah, there's hope for you yet! How about Hebrew Nationals. Do you eat Hebrew Nationals?"

What's a Hebrew National?" I asked. This was getting worse by the moment. I considered leaving, but then I would have to pass that guard dog again.

"Oh sweet Jesus! Where did you grow up? Who raised you? You don't know what a Hebrew National is? What kind of a Jew are you?"

Now I was angry. "I am a Jew that left the temple at age eight. And no I don't know what a Hebrew National is, and how do you know I am Jewish? I don't feel Jewish or think Jewish, so how do you know that?"

"A Hebrew National is the BEST hotdog on the planet. Have you ever been to New York City? Any good vender who knows his butt from a hole in his head would be selling Hebrew Nationals. With sauerkraut and mustard. A little bit of heaven, right here on earth. Everyone knows that."

Patricia sat silent for a moment, waiting.

"Yep, best hotdogs on the planet." The right foot drew slow circles in the air, showing off tiny perfectly-painted bright red toenails.

I was surprised at my own anger and sat back on the sofa, trying to get my bearings. I had been looking forward to meeting this woman for weeks. The first time I called, I had been told that Patricia was in the hospital and would not be doing any work for months. So I waited three months before calling again. That time Patricia herself had answered and scheduled this session.

All I knew then was that Patricia was an Irish healer who had been adopted into the Pine Ridge Lakota by Ione Badcob.

The adoption ceremony gave Patricia status in the tribe as Ione's adopted sister, and Patricia was welcome to visit and take part in ceremonies, and was treated with great respect as a tribe member when she was there. Members of the tribe regularly visited Patricia at her home on Mt. Hood., and she had close ties with the Lakota Indians on the Pine Ridge Reservation. I knew that Patricia taught the Rounds, year-long courses on the teachings of the Lakota Medicine Wheel, to groups of women.

I had been looking forward to this day with hope: hope that maybe I had found someone who could make sense of the angels I saw, the sounds I sometimes heard, the dreams of things happening before they happened, the spirits I saw now and then. Someone who could help me find my spiritual ground.

Now, as I sat quietly, I realized that I was angry because Patricia didn't look like a healer. I hadn't known I had a preconceived idea of what a healer would look like, but I knew it wasn't this. Breath by breath, slowly calming, I was drawn to the warmth this woman gave out. It was something palpable, like a very odd—and a bit twisted—version of Glinda the Good Witch in *The Wizard of Oz*.

"Look, I know you are Jewish because of your last name. I assumed it. Honey, I am so glad you are here. I have been waiting to meet you since you called me, and I really am happy to see you. Let's begin. Tell me your story. All of it." Patricia turned on the tape recorder and waited.

I talked for two and a half hours, nonstop. I had never done this before, but now it just poured out, the entire story of my life up to that point.

Patricia listened, nodding in acknowledgment, twirling her right foot in a clockwise direction. I told of my childhood, my adolescence, my discovery of myself as a sexual being, my total lack of modeling for how to take care of myself, my numerous boyfriends and relationship casualties, my son, my experiences with violence, my travels, the magic of nature. My abilities to see another world, hear other sounds, all of it.

Then she spoke. "I can work with you. You have a good, strong spirit. But it's hard work. Hard work. It's going to take awhile. And don't do this work thinking it will undo the trauma. Do this work because your spirit needs it."

"Okay," I said. "Great. What's next?" In the telling of my story, I had felt connected with Patricia. Patricia made so few interruptions, and the quality of the healer's deep listening made me less aware of the physical person and more aware of the compassion held in Patricia's body.

"Next is…. I need about three weeks to go over all of this, and you come back and get on that massage table and I am going to take a look at your energy and see what I see. And my daughter will likely be here helping me. And the dog knows you now, so that will be easy. And I will have some chocolate for you, honey. Congratulations on staying alive!"

It was the beginning of a 13-year relationship, one that would change me, and my life, forever.

When I returned to have Patricia "take a look at my energy"….whatever that meant, I noticed upon arriving that Sheba the dog remained relaxed and lying down. I couldn't believe she would remember me from three weeks ago, but as I got out of my car, she neither rose nor barked.

Patricia greeted me at the door. "Hi, Sweetie!" she smiled at me as though I was the best thing since Swiss cheese. "See, she remembered you, honey!" She was looking healthier, had more color in her round cheeks, and was wearing an actual dress. "Go on into the healing room. Get on the massage table. I'll be right in. Oh, there's some chocolate in there for you!"

I entered the healing room and was struck with beauty of it. All the sacred objects, the light coming through the windows, the cedar guardian trees outside. Indeed, there was a chocolate bar there on the table. I laughed.

I lay on the buffalo skin which covered the massage table, feeling the warmth and power of it.

Shannon, Patricia's daughter, came quietly into the room. I looked over and saw a beautiful young woman, wearing a simple dress and a shawl, with eyes that reminded me of a cat.

"Hi," she extended her hand, "I'm Shannon. I'm going to assist Mom. You can lie back down."

There was something about Shannon I liked immediately.

She knew about boundaries. She didn't spend a lot of time trying to make small talk, or being sure I was fine. She just got on with it. Patricia entered, and sat at the head of the massage table and placed her hands near my head. Her hands gave off so much heat that I felt like I was falling into a warm half-asleep, partially-dreaming state, and had no memory of time passing till I heard Patricia speak.

"Come sit on the couch, honey. Slowly. Here, Shannon will help you."

I sat. Shannon left, first handing Patricia a paper that I couldn't read. I waited while Patricia made herself comfortable, adjusted her shawl, her reading glasses, looked at some notes she had made as well as at the paper from Shannon.

Patricia began to speak.

"This is not pretty. I honestly don't quite know how you have stayed alive. I only can guess it's the strength of your soul, because other than that, you pretty much nearly did die as a baby. I have never seen anything quite like this. You have a baby tucked way inside your uterus. I don't mean a real baby, but the energy of a baby who is so frightened she won't come out. She is hiding in there."

She went on to describe problems with my eyesight and my hearing stemming from my infant terror and trauma, continually saying, "It's a wonder you are alive."

She identified energy from WWII beating around me, the

energy of fear and the horrors done by the Nazis that had become a part of my energy field. She said that I had never had a safe night's sleep in my life. That I didn't really know what the word "safe" means.

Patricia went on to say that my third eye was too open, so my dreamtime is every bit as intense as waking time, but I have no control over dreamtime. She said, "You are also psychic, highly intuitive, and see angels and spirits and always have, and I think maybe this is part of what has saved you."

She described the illnesses I had as a child, the high fevers, and visits to the Spirit World that were a way of my guides helping me. That was the only time she could see my mother caring for me in a loving way, when the fevers became really high. In a way, she told me, these illnesses saved me because I escaped the reality of my house.

Then she said, "Your energy in your abdomen is all frozen up. You have no way of running energy through your pelvis or down your legs into the earth. And your heart has felt like it was bleeding because of deep damage when you were born, not physical damage. You were born with your nervous system on the outside and your home was not soft or comforting or safe, so your heart worked overtime. You felt with your heart, and you felt too much. That's why your ears closed down. Also your father's screaming was too much for you as a baby. You thought you were going to die.

"But," she said, "You have a really strong soul. You are a very wise, old soul and this has helped you stay alive. You are a warrior. Stubborn as they come, but that has helped you stick to what you know to be true. The remarkable thing is that, although energetically you are a bit of a train wreck, you are also one of the most 'on your path' people I have ever met. Remarkable."

Patricia paused to take a deep breath. "You are going to need one doozy of a surgery, dear," she told me. "The full deal. We will take the baby out, and close up the heart, right your third eye, get rid of the energy of the war around you, help you connect with the earth and sky. Fix your hearing. But you have a lot of preparing to do. For one thing, you have to put on at least five pounds, hopefully ten. Right now you are too thin to survive it.

"And for another, you have no way of flushing energy through your system. So you tend to collect emotions and they just get stuck and recycle through you, and I can't work on that till you do some work yourself first."

I listened to all of this with two minds. One was that everything Patricia was saying made complete sense to me, and felt deeply true. The other mind said that it had to be a made-up story, that my childhood could not have been that bad. And yet, I had not one good memory of it. But then I became aware that my body had let go of some tension, releasing a palpable flow of energy throughout my body. I had a sense of relief, of finally having heard the truth. And I hadn't died from it. I was sitting, just taking it in, sitting and breathing.

"The good news," said Patricia, "Is that we can do this. And it won't just be healing for you. It will be healing backwards and forward in time, and other members of your family will feel it too. You are going to have to be brave, willing, and you have a lot of work to do."

Patricia told me it would take about four years of work before I was strong enough to have such a surgery. So I began.

It took a full four years to prepare my mind and body and spirit for my surgery. During those four years, Patricia sent me out into nature to learn my lessons. I walked barefoot throughout the trails of the Columbia River Gorge, on rocks, snowy hills, in rivers. I learned to connect through my feet deep into the earth. I learned to concentrate on the soft, cool parts of the sole of my foot, not the jagged points where rocks pierced. Patricia waited till I learned one lesson before going on to the next. Sometimes this was a matter of days, weeks, or months.

She sent me to visit with my spirit animals, real animals that had lessons to teach me. All the learning was in nature, with great respect for all life.

She taught me to cleanse with sage, and to pray out loud to Creator. She sent me to different areas of the mountains to learn the energies of the North, South, East, and West.

Patricia never accompanied her students, as she was too heavy. She also believed that a person had to learn for themselves.

There was no substitute for going into nature and opening oneself to the lessons. She taught me how to protect myself. I always carried a knife, sage, and tobacco, and prayed for protection.

Patricia told me stories of how the buffalo always stood strong and faced the snowstorms, looking directly into them with the knowledge that Buffalo had the strength to survive. She told me this once when I arrived in tears from a broken relationship with a man. I felt as if my spirit, not my heart, was broken. Patricia sent me to lie on the buffalo skin, and I lay there crying and crying, clinging to it.

There is no feeling like a buffalo skin. It holds the energy of the animal, and I always felt that something with enormous heart filled with wisdom came into the room when I lay on that skin. He became one of my guides, this presence, and that time he told me, "No man, no human can break you. Spirit does not break." I did not understand at the time, but I did many years later.

Once, when Patricia sent me to the woods for the night in hopes of meeting one of my medicine animals, I broke down crying. I returned to her house to say I could not do it; the woods scared me. She gave me chocolate and sent me outside to sleep in her teepee, telling me to come in if I got scared. She made sure I had plenty of blankets, and told me, "You can't learn anything if you're frightened. You first have to learn how to step into love, not fear, because you can't stand in the two at the same time."

My learning was done without the use of any drugs, ingestion of plants, or any substance. The only substance was Mother Earth and my connection with Earth and Sky. It was and continues to be a never-ending chipping away of fear and replacing that powerful vibration with the only stronger vibration in the universe, that of love.

People came from all over the world to Patricia's healing room. Those who experienced surgery left with a new sense of the world, themselves, and their lives. They had been taken to their core, through their ancestral lines, to the seed of themselves, and been brought back clean, new, with only their own karma to work out.

After participating in ceremonies to unite me with my soul, I received my true name, owning and releasing the pain I had caused up to that time in my life. Taking vows to protect and heal, I was finally ready, after four years, for my own surgery.

For the next 12 years Patricia taught me to be part of a team who assisted her with psychic surgeries. She would travel out of her body and into the spirit world at speeds that made me dizzy. Other times she would move so slowly, I felt I would collapse before the surgeries ended. During these operations I would look into her eyes and see she was gone. I could only hang on for dear life as I felt her tug at my being for grounding. I will never forget the time I looked into her eyes and saw nothing but two black holes, and fully understood that she was in no way present. It was the first time I understood in my body what it is to witness travel into Spirit World.

She could be quite fierce, especially during surgeries, giving instructions: "You close your eyes during this and you die, end of story." She meant it too.

When I assisted with the psychic surgeries, learning to work with the rocks and crystals, feathers and other elements of the healing tradition, I experienced the source of both light and darkness in the world, but most importantly the never-changing light, goodness, and love of Creator. This is rooted in faith, in the discovery and experience of the exquisite order of the natural universe. This came to me in deep silence and changed me forever. I know that one candle in a universe of darkness is more powerful than all the blackness that surrounds. I know that we come from and return to pure love, and that it is here within us with every breath we take. I had found the remedy for the aching in my soul.

Patricia was a huge presence in every form, physical as well as spiritual. And she was filled with contradictions. When she wasn't healing, she loved watching her big-screen TV, especially the Academy Awards which we celebrated each year. We'd dress up in our Hollywood best, prepare fancy sugar-filled munchies, and critique each celebrity as they passed by on her flat screen TV. "Who let you out of the house?" she would exclaim as some poor, overly-groomed actor approached the microphone.

"Gorgeous, absolutely gorgeous. What a rock on her hand!" Patricia delivered opinions as a queen would declare policy from her living room throne and we'd laugh so hard our gowns would split.

Her bathroom was filled with pink angel soap and the bathtub her husband had made for her that allowed her to see the forest outside. She loved nothing more than soaking and playing in rose-scented bubble bath with her collection of rubber ducks.

She could scream, "Eat shit and die!" during an argument and laugh so hard in the same breath her belly contracted and shook. She was big in every way.

Patricia died from a rare type of lung cancer. I had no illusions that she was perfect: not a Buddha, not a Mary, not a Christ in female form, yet I saw in her eyes and heart a love big enough to encompass the universe. I always recognized her humanness and vulnerability, yet found within her an amazing teacher and friend. For this I am forever grateful. I also believe that her death was related to the work she had been doing for so many years. She did not always protect herself well, and she sometimes worked when she was tired. I believe this left her vulnerable; all those surgeries took their toll. And yet, I don't know that she would have done anything differently.

Some years before her death I asked permission to practice healing in my own form and she gave me her full support. She stood beside me in her kitchen, to the right and slightly behind me. I remember her voice: "Just call my name and I'll be there with you, shoulder to shoulder." This was important to me. It was her way of saying she trusted me to heal with integrity. There have been times I have called on her during healings, and that smile of hers that spread from ear to ear comes to mind. I see those rosy cheeks and hear her say, "Hi, honey." I am forever indebted to her for teaching me what unconditional love is, and for all the lessons from Mother Earth.

IN THE SURGERY ROOM

We stood planted around the massage table, ready to begin the psychic surgery for the woman who lay on a soft sheet over a buffalo skin, and covered with another blanket. Patricia held court, seated at the head of table, and the three of us on the surgery team stood poised for action.

The client had already laid out her soul bundle, a collection of natural materials in honor of her soul, as well as pictures of her family, candles, materials for prayer ties, and personal treasures at the altar. That had given us a couple of hours to catch glimpses of her life, but there was never any rush or sense of linear time in this process of laying out the altar in preparation for the surgery.

In much the same way that doctors work in sterile environments, we had sealed this room with sage, prayers, and candles, candies for the stuffed bears, and prayer ties in the four directions, as well as protective ties surrounding us on the outer landscape.

The surgery room was built by Patricia's husband, and was filled with wondrous sacred objects, mostly from Lakota traditions. Outside, the tall pines, hemlock, and cedar stood as collective guardians. We were surrounded by gorgeous, vast Northwest landscapes, greeted with beauty in all directions.

This surgery was to remove dark energy, familial disease that had been passed from one generation to the next and had taken energetic form in her body. The disease resonated physically and in terms of the relationships in her life, and she had come to Patricia resolved to do whatever was necessary.

Our tools were drums, feathers, rocks, candles, song, and sacred objects. Our main surgeon was Patricia, who gave us directives. Our protection was well honed and strong, as we all knew that certain energies did not like the removal of darkness and in fact, rebelled against it. This could take the form of a physical attack, or a psychic/spiritual attack, and Patricia had trained us all in being well protected.

We entered these surgeries knowing they were dangerous and highly intense. We had been called to assist in them, and we had to leave all egos—really, everything that might result in discord during the work—at the door. We stood only to serve the soul of the person lying on the table.

In preparation, Patricia had listened to the life story of this client, and made a diagram of the energy flow and blocks in her body. She had worked with her daughter, mapping out what needed to be done, and just like an allopathic surgeon, they had prepared the patient with pre-op and post-op instructions.

The singing began, officially opening the surgery, and we entered another world—one of spirits, urgency, utter calm, endless possibility. A world of mean spirits, light spirits, horrible dark energies that wound like snakes trying to strangle. We began painting the woman's body with clay that both shielded her and prepared her to be opened.

There was always singing as we painted, as though nothing was happening out of the ordinary, just a beautiful song. But it was a calling to the spirits. The songs were shields, as well as entryways to open the directions and ask for help. At the same time, Patricia had her hands lightly on the woman, administering what I can only call an "energetic anesthesia".

We brought platters of various crystals and stones to Patricia, removing them from the shelves in the surgery room, presenting them like hors d'oeuvres at a dinner party. Patricia chose which to use and told us where to place them on and around the woman.

Patricia directed me to take out my knife and showed me where to cut. Although I did not cut into the woman's physical body, I cut into her energetic body, carefully, with a hand that did not tremble or shake. Another assistant stood by me with a bowl, and collected the mess that came oozing out of the wound.

I nearly threw up. (We had a bucket in the room for this purpose because it was not unusual for one of us to need it.) Energy has odors, and some are repugnant.

At the same time, Patricia urgently pointed to the floor, saying "snakes, snakes!" and told one of the assistants to cut the heads off the snakes. She began chopping away at them.

I was directed to begin drumming hard and fast and I stood facing the north and drummed as hard as I could but steady, with no change in the rhythm. Patricia signaled for me to continue. The client was shaking all over, and now assistants were covering her with blankets and larger rocks so she would not leave her body.

Patricia showed me where the dark spirit was going to emerge and told me to get ready. She told me I had one chance and one chance only. I nodded, still drumming, leaning in close to her ear to hear her. Then I stopped drumming, picked up my knife and waited for her signal.

There was no hesitating. When the spirit emerged, it flew at me and I pierced it in the throat, its only vulnerable place. It lay in a heap on the floor. Now it was my turn to shake, and assistants poured water on me, and on we went.

In moments like these, I sometimes found myself in two places at once. One was totally engaged in the reality of the surgery. Another was almost standing outside, looking in, and thinking "What the hell are these crazy women doing in there?" I had spoken with Patricia about this, and she was aware of it. She had told me, "Never lose your skepticism. It is one of your most valuable gifts. It keeps you balanced." I loved her for this.

One of the assistants was a man, and he fought with the last spirit who tried to interfere with the healing.

We poured light into the woman. We took feathers and with loud sounds, we pushed the light into her. Around her. Above and below. We sang lullabies, songs of sweetness, Amazing Grace. We stood in silence. Removing all the rocks and crystals that had been lying on her, and placing them all in a container to be washed later, we stood around her and sent light into her body.

More songs, more silence. Patricia prayed long and softly. Her prayers included the winged ones, the two-legged, the four-legged, those behind the iron gates, those who lived within the earth, the ancestors, All Our Relations.

A long silence.

Patricia instructed the woman to ask her soul if it was done. If anything else needed to be done. Five hours had passed, seven since the woman had first entered the room. It was complete. The woman whispered 'Yes, it is done."

We helped her up, slowly, and into a room where her new clothing lay, the clothing that she had brought for after her surgery, and helped her to dress. She would wear the clay paint for three days and nights. And she would go home and rest and be assisted, just as if she had had a physical surgery. She would be weak and very sore all over her body and would need caring for.

Then, over time, she would experience a huge shift in her stance in the world. She would stand in the center of her own power, with only this lifetime to work out. Many clients needed a year to integrate this energetic shift, and most were grateful for the rest of their lives.

I was so happy to be a part of these surgeries. Through them, I learned to work with crystals, rocks, sounds, drums, singing, and to be part of a true team. I also learned about dark energies, their power, and how to protect myself.

Patricia had told me never to look into her eyes during a surgery, but once I forgot and I looked straight at her. I felt like I was being sucked into her eyes. It was as though no one was in there, just pure energy and a dark windy tunnel leading to infinite space with great speed and massive potential for shifting energies, like being pulled into the eye of a storm, lost. I jerked my head away just in time.

In that moment, I realized that Patricia was gone, totally not present. It was the first time I had seen a shaman at work, really understood the nature of the journey, although Patricia would never have called herself a shaman.

But that leave-taking, complete absence and that feeling of rapidly rushing energy into a vortex of space...years later I would come to know that for myself. What I have never known is how Patricia was able to return to her body seemingly without help. I suspect it was the presence of her daughter that allowed her to self-locate.

In all the eight years that I assisted Patricia, I never once felt truly unsafe. To this day I am deeply grateful for that work. I honestly don't know anyone else on the planet who does that work in her particular manner: Patricia was one of a kind in so many ways. And there was that smile at the end of a surgery, from ear to ear, with her red painted lips, as she sparkled and said, "Well done, ladies and gentlemen."

DEATH AT PINE RIDGE

When I first met Patricia, she told me that she was part Irish, part Lakota. I assumed that meant she was part Lakota by bloodline, but it turned out that Patricia had gone through a traditional adoption ceremony at the Pine Ridge Reservation in South Dakota. Her sister Ione Badcob, a full blooded Lakota, was then considered Patricia's sister in every way. Many years later I learned that this adoption ceremony is viewed differently now than it may once have been, and that full-blooded members of the tribe regarded it with varying degrees of acceptance. But when I knew her, Patricia was included at the table, literally and figuratively, when we were at the reservation, and treated with all the respect any elder tribal member was shown.

Patricia developed and taught The Rounds, teachings that were mostly Lakota, inspired by her experiences in the native community. The four directions and basic understanding of them, tobacco ties, prayers, moontime, respect, giveaway, and sweat lodges were all Lakota. Patricia wanted a native pipe carrier to oversee the sweats to make sure they were respectful and kept traditional, and she had heard about Don Moccasin, a native Assiniboine, from a mutual native friend, so she called him up, invited him out, and showed him her program. He signed on and started the sweat lodges. Lakota teachings were woven through the program, which is why Ione, from the Pine Ridge Reservation, was comfortable there. Ione visited often and shared freely.

The medicine man at Pine Ridge was Ione's cousin. The ceremony he did was usually just called "doctoring." People went for doctoring and got whatever treatment he chose. Patricia had been present at more than one "doctoring." and participated fully in many of the traditions of the Lakota. She spent a good deal of time at Pine Ridge and visited with Ione frequently.

My connection with Ione was mostly from a distance, watching her and listening to her during The Rounds at Patricia's, but Ione and I had enjoyed a few conversations in private, and I loved talking with her. She had a straightforward way with words, using as few as needed to say only what needed to be said. She helped me trust myself and my intuition on a couple of occasions. I loved her deeply lined face, and her command of language, as well as her amusement with the women who came to the Rounds. Ione sometimes just sat, quietly shaking her head in bewilderment at some of the questions, a wry smile on her face.

Ione Badcob died of complications from diabetes, a common illness on the reservation. I went to Pine Ridge with Patricia, Shannon, and another friend for Ione's funeral. It was my first time there.

We arrived after a two-day drive in Patricia's van across too many miles, at times surrounded by Harley Davidson motorcyclists, since a Harley convention was also happening in South Dakota. They were our companions on the highway, the engines sounding like off-key throat singing.

I did not know what to expect on the reservation, since no one had told me much, so I was open. But I did not expect the level of poverty we encountered, or the commitment to ceremony that remained intact despite the grueling physical realities of existence there.

The land is powerful, and you can feel a palpable sense of its bloody and violent history as soon as you enter. I saw Stronghold Table, a mesa that was the location of the last Ghost Dances. In fact, it was the U.S. authorities' attempt to repress this movement that eventually led to the Wounded Knee Massacre on December 29, 1890. A mixed band of Lakota and Sioux, led by Chief Spotted Elk, sought sanctuary at Pine Ridge after fleeing the Standing Rock Agency, where Sitting Bull had been killed during efforts to arrest him. The families were intercepted by a heavily armed detachment of the Seventh Cavalry, which attacked them, killing many women and children as well as warriors. This was the last large engagement between U.S. forces and Native Americans.

I could write a book on the history of the division of the sacred Black Hills, but suffice it to say that the US government not only backed out of its original treaty regarding the Black Hills, but it forcibly repossessed parts of it for mining and development.

As of 2007, Pine Ridge had an unemployment rate of 80-90%, a per capita income of $4,000, eight times the United States rate of diabetes, five times the United States rate of cervical cancer, twice the rate of heart disease, eight times the United States rate of tuberculosis, an alcoholism rate estimated as high as 80%, with one in four infants born with fetal alcohol syndrome or the effects of alcoholism. The suicide rate is more than twice the national rate, teen suicide rate four times the national rate, infant mortality three times the national rate. Life expectancy on Pine Ridge is the lowest in the United States.

As we entered the reservation, it was clear to me, even from the van, that there were places there where you wouldn't want to travel alone, places that were unsafe, as if the current reality was only thinly overlying a dangerous and brutal past.

On the first day of our visit, we were invited into the home of a woman who knew Patricia. As we stepped from the van onto the prairie and gravel drive, we could hear the voice of the winds. They seemed to carry with them all the violence and sorrow that has taken place there. Patricia had described people freezing to death in this place in winter, as the land was wide open to snow and wind, and the houses offered poor shelter. I could easily imagine it.

When we entered the small house, I did my best to hide my shock at the utter chaos: a mess of garbage, clothing, toys, and furniture scattered throughout the place. Ants crawled over piles of clothing and dishes. It was as though the winds had blown through, destroying all sense of order.

Patricia and her daughter were acting as if this was normal, so I pretended not to notice. As the woman flung clothing and trash off the chairs and we were invited to sit, I looked out the window at the expansive land, and wondered how it had come to this.

We were staying some forty minutes off the reservation, where there was a Holiday Inn, a Walmart, and other middle-America consumer-driven establishments. The contrast was disturbing, disorienting, and somehow deeply revealing of our history on this land. As I stood at the window, sadness took hold of me and I could not keep up with the conversation. No one seemed to notice or care, and the next thing I knew, we were on our way to the gymnasium. I had these blank times of getting lost in sadness several times at Pine Ridge, where the conversation seemed to flow into the background and all I could feel was the pain of the people.

During the Rounds, Ione had told me more than once that the Elders of the tribe meant it when they prayed for All Our

Relations, meaning that this prayer included All Our White Relations. More than once I had asked Ione how this could be, and she had just shrugged and looked at me. "All our relations including you," she had said. I could not apologize for being of Russian Jewish heritage and white-skinned, nor did I want to. But the sadness I felt was painful.

The gymnasium had been converted to a ceremonial place for Ione's funeral, and she was lying in an open casket. Members of the tribe came to pay respects, leave offerings, photos, blankets, giveaways. A circle of men pounded away at their drums, singing in high pitched tones that permeated the room, the building, and the air outside.

We were in the gymnasium most of the day, watching as chairs were placed for the service, colorful tribal members coming and going, mostly dressed in everyday garments, but a few in more ceremonial clothing. Ione's cousin, the man who did the doctoring, was there, as were many elders. Patricia sat with them, visiting, listening, laughing.

I was struck by the naturalness of death in this setting. Nothing was hidden from the children. Death was a part of life, not some secret to be hidden away, or feared, or kept from them. People went about their lives in the midst of death in a way that I had never witnessed, and it was comforting.

Pictures of Ione and other family members stood at the front of the gymnasium. Gorgeous handmade star quilts were hung in her honor. Gifts for her family were brought. The movement and energy was lively, not sad.…not tragic, but rather as if to say, "This is what we do when someone dies."

Children bounced about, ran up to the casket, and touched the body curiously, then ran to their parents with comments. Ione's foot was gangrened, and there was a smell coming from the casket. Nothing was really hidden, except a bit of her foot.

I had a sense of being in a highly-charged atmosphere, a collision of realities. The tribe had a strong current of spiritual strength in the face of unconscionable treatment by the US government. People lived in poverty that was below Third World standards, succumbing to the freezing winter winds, with roofs that were sometimes no more than tarps against the below-freezing temperatures. Alcoholism was rampant, especially among the youth, and the rubble that people lived in was almost blinding in its chaos.

Yet in the midst of this, the elders gathered at tables to share stories, the drummers drummed and sang, preparations for the next day's funeral were taking place and lives flowed on with threads of ancient wisdom wending their way into the modern-day building of brick and stone.

The funeral ceremony began the next day. Most of the people had made me feel neither welcome nor unwelcome; I was simply trying to take it all in. We sat on folding chairs, and the funeral ceremony was an odd mixture of Lakota and Christian ideology, symbology, and prayer. At the end, the chairs were pushed back, and everyone stood to make a serpentine line. Not sure whether to join in or not, I glanced at Patricia's daughter who nodded yes.

Person by person, we passed one another and touched hands as an acknowledgment. No one looked me in the eye, and I remembered this from the Rounds, that a usual native greeting was not an exchange of energy. I just felt honored that they would include me at all. The ceremony faded as I was overcome with sadness again, and the next thing I remember was standing outside and watching Ione's simple casket being lifted onto a flatbed pulled by horses. We made our way up a hill to the graveyard, which had flowers wound through the fence in her honor. Children were encouraged to throw flowers on the casket, and other members of the tribe did the same as she was laid to rest and the men began the work of covering the casket.

The wind picked up; the sun was beginning to set, and I felt out of time. The scene itself was timeless: the passage of an Elder. The memories and traditions of the people were passed down verbally and with each elder's death, another voice was lost. Stories and wisdom, lost. The real knowledge of the Sundance and other ceremonies, dying.

I was totally exhausted as we made our way back into the gymnasium, but it was now my turn to help in the kitchen, to help serve the fry bread and jam, the feast after the funeral. As I worked alongside the other women, for the first time I received smiles and pats on the back, welcoming gestures. Some test had been passed. I served till I literally could not stand up any longer, and slipped out to the van to go to sleep.

The next morning, Patricia's daughter Shannon, my friend Karen, and several others of us went into town to a shop that sold native jewelry. The shop was filled with so many authentic, beautiful things. But as I stood there, I suddenly felt as if I was literally turning into stone, unable to move. I signaled to Patricia's daughter, and she took one look at me, and said to the others "Let's go NOW." They half carried me into the van, where I sat like a statue, back to the hotel. They carried me into the room, laid me down on the floor, and Karen and Shannon began to work on me energetically.

I remember Shannon saying something like "Your plumbing is backed up. You soaked up everyone's grief." I began sobbing and sobbing, which lasted a long time till I was completely cried out. Patricia was in the room visiting with a few people from the reservation and she leaned over from where she sat to watch.

"I didn't know you were going to have a nervous breakdown on us," she joked. I lay there thinking, "Very funny. Very, very funny," but that was Patricia. Then she came over, patted me on the back, and told me I would be fine.

"What the hell was that?" I asked Shannon afterward.

"Well, you just soaked up all the grief in the room and that combined with your own grief….it had no way to get out." I lay on the floor of the hotel room a long time. Images from that line of touching everyone's hand went through my mind. Images of Ione in her casket, the children running up to her. The procession up to the burial ground. The wind. The hovel of a house. Fry bread and jam. All mixed in my mind like the chaos on the floor of the home we had visited. I slept.

As we drove back to Oregon, it occurred to me that I had not seen one bird, one animal the whole time on the reservation, other than the horses leading the flatbed with the casket, and the ants in the house. It struck me as odd. In the vast landscape, not one bird in flight. Nothing.

Maybe my eyes weren't trained to see in that landscape. Or maybe I hadn't had enough time. But it was so unusual. It's the only time in my life I can remember being on such vast land and not seeing animal life. To this day, it's a mystery to me.

BAREFOOT HIKING

As part of my training to connect with the earth, Patricia has suggested I go barefoot whenever and wherever possible, including on my hikes. The Columbia River Gorge offers fantastic hikes amidst a grandeur of forest and waters that still have a wilderness feel to them. On the west coast there are no in-holdings, so the likelihood of coming across any human structure once into a hike is practically zero.

I considered the Columbia River Gorge my backyard, and hiked at least twice a week, on long and often steep trails over rocky, sandy, wet, and dirt terrain. My feet were hoof-like at this point from hiking barefoot over such a variety of surfaces. I had learned how to relax and rocks no longer bothered me. I had long ago become used to the stares of others I met along the trails, noticing my bare feet. "Did you see that woman?" they would say immediately upon passing me, as if now out of sight, I didn't exist. "She didn't have any shoes on! That's nuts! "

I had become aware of the big industry of hiking boots, and other outdoor gear deemed necessary, as I hiked with less and less over the course of the year. The comments no longer really reached my ears, and long ago I stopped making eye contact with anyone on any trail, as my intention was to be in and with nature, not people.

I had come to a time when I really could not imagine putting anything on between my feet and the earth. I had indeed learned to bring the heat of the earth up into my body through my feet, as Patricia had told me I would. No matter the weather, rain or shine, I was barefoot. Eventually I could hike in patches of snow as well, though never through significant amounts for long. I needed less outer wear as my feet grew tougher.

I loved the lightness of being barefoot and the knowledge

of the terrain beneath my feet. I felt more alive, more connected with whatever trail I was on, and my mind had long ago quieted the moment I stepped onto trails.

One of the moments I always loved was coming upon a stream and stepping into it and feeling the relief of the cold water. Hiking barefoot had also transformed my ability, not only to endure cold mountain water, but to love it. If I was near a stream that was far from people, I could lie naked, immersed in the water, and feel merged with the flow. Happy. This was my happiness. The two years I spent learning to get my feet literally on the ground improved my overall health, my attitude, and my joy in being among the trees and creatures, watching the clouds transform and feeling at home on my own and far from people.

On one particular afternoon, I was returning from a steep, difficult hike in the mountains near Bend, Oregon. I had started out early, at sunrise, and had failed to bring sufficient water. About a third of the way down the dirt, rocky trail, I realized I was both tired and thirsty and had made a mistake. I knew I was unlikely to meet anyone, as this was a little-used, difficult trail, and it was past mid autumn.

The expression "girded my loins" came to mind as I made my way down. I had placed a couple of pebbles under my tongue to produce saliva. As I trotted along, something in my body shifted, as though a wave of energy passed through me. I suddenly felt very deer, for lack of a better way to describe the sensation. My feet felt like true hooves; my legs light and unstoppable and easily able to negotiate the never-ending downhill terrain. All sense of thirst was gone and my eyesight was bright and clearer than usual. I could smell the forest in a way I never had before, pine, cedar and hemlock wafting on waves of mountain air. My gait changed to a swifter stride, and a jolt of electric shock went through me as I detected "human" and jumped off the trail into the woods.

A man and his two sons wearing backpacks headed up the trail.

"Hurry up," the man said. "We're losing light."

"Wait!" said one of the boys. He was looking through the trees, directly at me. "I see a deer!"

"Come on. Don't stop. We need to make camp before dark."

They continued along the trail. The boy looked back. I waited till they had rounded the curve in the trail.

Immediately I began nearly running down the trail, feeling I had narrowly missed some harm. All I remember the whole way down, reaching my car just at dark, was the rhythm of my hoofs. Upon seeing my car, all sense of animal vanished in an instant, and there I stood, thirsty, tired, and happy I had left some water in the car.

When I was next at Patricia's, I told her about this hike and asked what she thought.

She was quiet a long time, her right foot twirling round and round.

"Well, it's hard to say. But it's a good thing you were

barefoot, deer."

I laughed.

"No really," she said. "This being hunting season and all, you were lucky."

That was as much as she ever said about it.

I know now that sometimes, when the need is great, it is possible to occupy the form of another. For me, it happens very rarely, maybe three times now in a lifetime. And I can say that I have met a couple of creatures who I knew to be humans in animal disguise.

KNEE-DEEP IN SHIT

I decided to sublet the top floor of the big house I rented. My landlord gave me permission, and the day the ad came out, I received a phone call from a woman named Mary. Could she come and see the place right away? I was anxious to rent it out, so I told Mary to come over.

The doorbell rang, and I opened the door to a woman in her mid-40s, somewhat disheveled, but not alarmingly so. Still, some deep intuitive sense told me something was off—but this was overruled by Mary's love of the place and my own desire to rent it out as soon as possible.

Mary's first move was to wall off the upper indoors doorway with plastic, claiming that the cigarette smoke from downstairs was harmful to her and she could smell it upstairs. Her next move was to announce that she had a severe form of cancer and was receiving no treatment, but was eating a macrobiotic diet. On her next visit, Mary asked if there was any way she could get some pills so she could commit suicide if the pain got too bad.

Obviously I should have listened to my intuition. I kept Mary away from my son Liam, and told her firmly that I was not going to be supplying any medications to her and that her health concerns were her own business.

Next came a succession of boyfriends, each one weirder than the next. They all looked undernourished and creepy, and none of them lasted with Mary more than three weeks. It became clear to me that I needed to get Mary out, as she was beginning to practice some bizarre rituals around the house, including ringing bells and loudly chanting incantations at all hours of the night. Perhaps the cancer had gone to her brain. Torn between wanting to be compassionate to this stranger upstairs, and angry that Mary had not told the truth from the start, I gave her a 30-day notice of eviction. And then it began.

Daily, I heard drilling sounds upstairs, sometimes going on far into the night. One of the ex-boyfriends arrived with bags full of god knows what and left empty-handed. When the day came that Mary was supposed to move, she didn't. This required going to court and taking further action to get her out.

Mary's response was to stay one more month. When she finally left, she did so at midnight.

I went to look upstairs. The door was locked. I heard water running. I called the police, saying I needed help getting into the upper part of my home. They arrived and, using various tools, they opened the door, cutting through layers of plastic on the inside of the doorway. Water was beginning to run down the stairs. "What the hell is going on here?" I said.

The upstairs was filled with trash, including animal feces and all manner of rotting food. Dozens of holes had been drilled in the walls, and there were hundreds of ladybugs on all the window sills. And notes, with drawings showing Mary's cancer seeping from her body into mine. Words painted on the walls: Bitch. Die Bitch. I could hardly breathe as I made my way from room to room, each room and every closet filled with trash and cat shit and some human feces as well.

I called the landlord and promised I would take full responsibility, but I wanted her to see what I was dealing with. We documented the damage. I hired a dumpster and a cleaning service and, donning a mask, rubber gloves, and a rubber suit, I worked with the crew. Two weeks and three thousand dollars later, the upstairs was physically clean. Two weeks after that, my brother was in town and offered to do a Buddhist ceremony to clean the place energetically.

After that final cleansing, I called Patricia, and told her the whole story. Patricia listened politely, adding the expected "Oh, how awfuls" and "sweet Jesus" and such. At the end there was a long pause and silence over the phone. Then Patricia said, "And the lesson is......?"

"The lesson," I replied, "is to follow my intuition."

"You got it!" laughed Patricia. "Otherwise you are going to be knee-deep in shit! Now go and pray your butt off for her." Patricia always got right to the point.

SHIELDS

I have completed my shields after six months of working on them, on and off. Although traditionally done on leather, Patricia asked me to do mine on poster board. She told me she imagined I would have quite a bit of work to do and probably wouldn't finish it this lifetime working on leather!

Shields are a way of looking at and taking responsibility for harm in one's life. I was told to write first the story of anyone who had caused me harm in my life, and to name that person and be clear about the harm caused. Along with the story, which was written on very large pieces of poster board, each filled with stories, were placed any objects related to the event. Including clothing, jewelry, anything.

These shields were to express all harm done to me over 38 years of my life. The writing of each story was done by hand, and objects were pinned, glued, and sewn onto the poster boards.

The next set of shields were the stories of all harm I had caused other people in those 38 years, again detailing the harm, naming the person, and attaching objects related to the incident.

The process had been at times nearly unbearable for me. I would work on one story, only to have three more arise that I hadn't thought of. About three months into the making of the shields I was sure that it was an infinite project and that Patricia was playing some cruel joke on me. I even called her to ask her if she was kidding me. Her answer was a brief "No, honey. Tell it like it is."

Some stories flowed out along with tears that softened the poster board temporarily. Others were laboriously written word by painful word. I could barely stand to look at the shields sometimes, and would hide them away in my closet, to begin again when I was ready.

The real shock came when I started looking at how many people I had hurt. I had no idea. Although I knew very well I had hurt people, to be truthful, I had not given it much thought. Nor regret. What happened while telling the stories was, of course, I realized that the pain I had caused them was no less than the pain I had received in my lifetime. Somehow I had held myself less accountable. It was not that I felt guilty; I simply GOT that I had really hurt people, intentionally or not.

In the end there were eight shields with all manner of things attached. A whole lot of hurt. A whole lot of stories. I put them in the back of the car and drove up to Patricia's, having told her I was ready. "Ready for what?" was my question, as she merely said, "Bring them up."

I had come to trust Patricia fully. It was not any one thing she did or said, but the whole of her. I just loved her. Fallible, stubborn, hilarious, and dead serious, she never let me down as a teacher. So I had long ago quit asking for explanations of things that I knew would make themselves clear in time.

As we sat in her living room in front of the fireplace, I was happy that the late autumn day brought damp cold that called for a hearthfire. Patricia was looking at the shields, sitting in her throne/chair, quietly weeping. "Oh my," she said. "Oh dear." Blowing her nose now and then. "Oh my my." This went on for a good half hour.

At the end of it, she rose, and said, 'OK, honey, stoke that fire up real good and sit in front of it and get prepared to put your shields in one at a time and watch the fire real close. Don't stop once you have started. I will be standing behind you, drumming. Do not look back at me. Keep your eyes on the fire and let's get these shields burnt."

I added logs to the fire, and sat with all my work at my side. I had become quite fond of these shields, no longer hiding them in the closet. Rather, I had displayed them in my bedroom and begun to look at them as some weird collage of pain; they had taken on interesting designs not of my intent. I had, I realized, befriended them. My reluctance to burn them surprised me, but as I placed the first one in the flames, and Patricia began drumming on her spider drum behind me, I knew in my body it was not only the right thing to do, there was no going back.

On and on we went. Into the fire. Drumming. Up in smoke. Objects burning. Clothing burning. Drumming. On and on. All the stories gone. All the stories up in smoke. More fire and more drumming. Patricia was singing, or someone was singing, and I lost track of my own actions and became entranced with the fire itself.

In the fire, dancing in a swift clockwise circle were all manner of animals. Coyotes, wolves, fox, bear. All dancing around in a large circle. More creatures joined the circle. Horses, frogs, butterflies and then....me. I was dancing with all the creatures round and round. We began to go faster and faster till we became one line of energy going round and round in the flames singing a happy song. A ridiculously happy song of life. Round and round in the flames singing. On and on, round and round, happy and singing. Singing the Happy Song.

I fell on my back laughing and laughing. Happier than I

could imagine being. Laughing and laughing. What a beautiful sight, dancing in the fire with all the Beings.

Slowly I came back into the room, coughing slightly and trying to figure out what I was doing on my back. The room was spinning slightly and I heard Patricia's voice from her chair. "Take your time, honey. You did good. Real good."

I sat up and the fire was nothing but embers. Staring in front of me, I had no idea what had just happened, but I felt lighter than I had ever felt in my life. Something was gone. Truly gone. I did not need to know what it was. I knew it wasn't returning.

Patricia brought me some chocolate and water. The chocolate tasted even better than usual.

"How about some buffalo?" she asked. Patricia knew I hated it when she suggested I eat meat, especially buffalo.

"Very funny," I replied.

"Hebrew National?" she asked.

"Haha."

"Just rest awhile," she said, indicating the couch and a blanket. I lay down and slept for three hours. Upon awakening, I sensed the same lightness immediately.

"Good work, honey. Real good. That's done," said Patricia. She hugged me. "You good to drive?" she asked.

"Oh I am good. Real good." In some way I cannot name, I have been real good ever since.

— PART II —

THE RAINFOREST

For years, I had longed to live in the Costa Rican rainforest. When she knew she was dying, Patricia encouraged me to go, telling me the trees would be my next teachers. I didn't know then that I would live there for five years as a healer, respected by the shamans of the nearby indigenous tribes.

THE

BIRTHDAY CAKE HOUSE

My home was at the top of a valley, and my back yard offered views down into the valley, over rainforest-covered hills, into the clouds. Rainbows began and ended on the mountaintop. Some afternoons, when I opened my front door a cloud would enter. Often, the trees outside were only dim shapes in the rainforest fog, and then bright sun would break through, revealing a sudden puzzle of light. My days were punctuated by the calls of shy, gorgeous birds that made themselves at home around the place.

The house was small, made of wood and concrete like most Tico houses, but I had painted the entire inside and outside of it myself, each wall a different primary color. The local people called it the Birthday Cake house, saying it looked very happy. Cracks in the floors and walls gave refuge to many beings: the walls were dotted with spiders, now and then a snake meandered through, an occasional tarantula found its way into the shower, and one evening a zorro, a cross between a possum and a rat, curled its skinny pink tail around the cold water faucet of my kitchen sink.

Despite the ever-present wildlife, it was the first time in my 55 years that I had felt truly at home. I heated the place with a beautiful old iron woodstove, and I hired a man to knock a window into one of the concrete-walled rooms to let the sun in.

The process was hilarious: the man covered in concrete pounding away at the wall, shouting "Que Puta!" ("What a whore!") as he worked. In one day, he had it done. Voila…a window. What a window!

My first attempts to learn Spanish were littered with comical mistakes. For instance, when I first arrived I had gone to the bank and asked for "cahones" – as in testicles – instead of "colones," money. And I had mistaken the word "cake" for "caca" … shit. At a gathering of neighbors, I thanked them for the piece of caca. They laughed and laughed. Oh well. I was improving.

People began to hear that I was a curandera, a healer woman, and they found their way to my Birthday Cake house, arriving at my bright pink door unannounced, always bringing an offering, no matter how modest. I was able to cure many people with a wide range of illnesses, but had to turn others away—a man hopping, his other leg broken, clutching a mango in one hand to offer as payment, a woman with a baseball-sized tumor bulging out the side of her neck—suggesting they go to the hospital, which I knew they could not afford. It broke my heart. Most were slight, thin, and muscular from farming or construction work. Few spoke any English. All were polite. By this time, I knew enough Spanish to hold a simple conversation. As long as no one ventured into physics or quantum theory, I could hold my own. But my lessons were just beginning.

THE
TREE PEOPLE

One day, as I walked through the rainforest, my day pack on my back, humming softly to myself, I noticed the beautiful patterns of sunlight reflected on the leaves. Like many days, I had planned to walk for several hours, immersing myself in bird song, in the many shades of green that were so impossibly beautiful, in the intricate wonders of the forest.

I came to one of my favorite places to sit, a large rock with a view of the trees all around, within earshot of a waterfall that produced a steady cascade of musical tones as it washed over the mountain.

Just before reaching into my pack for some water, I was startled by a sudden change in my consciousness. I thought I could see figures, just the outlines of human-like forms, emerging from the trees. I glanced at my hands to orient myself and looked again. There they were. The Tree People. When Patricia had referred to them, I had always assumed she was speaking metaphorically, acknowledging the wisdom of the trees.

But no, there I sat staring at what appeared to be outlines of human forms wavering slightly and connected to each tree, as though peeking out. I simply stared at them, and realized they were communicating with one another, conversing in some language I couldn't understand, and that they were aware of my presence.

They emerged in and out of the tree trunks, first showing themselves, and then hiding, in a slow wavy motion.

"Who are you?" I asked aloud.

"Tree spirits," came the answer, "And Old Spirits, of the Ancestors." The answers came in whispers to me, as though a soft breeze was blowing, though the air was still.

"Why can I see you?" I asked.

"We wanted to show ourselves to you. Just so you would know. That we exist. That we are alive. That we and the trees are one."

I didn't know what to say or do. So I simply sat there and witnessed them. The beauty of their forms was overwhelming, like some choreographed Martha Graham dance.

"Come and sit with us; we have stories to share. Not now, but one day. We are always here."

And with that, they disappeared. With a shiver, I was jolted back to normal consciousness and realized I was quite hungry and had broken into a sweat. I began drinking copious amounts of water from my container.

I did indeed return to the trees many times in the course of my years in Costa Rica, and I did hear the Tree Stories. Most of them are not to be shared, but here is one that should be.

Long ago, the forests rested. The Mother Tree in each group

watched over her children, watched them climb upwards towards the sky and witnessed the changes in seasons, the shift of the air, winds, rains. Now and then lightning caused one tree to split; the others tried to heal it, and sometimes they could and sometimes they could not.

When the people came, they did not recognize the trees as beings, only as some material to be used, and they began cutting them. The trees watched as their families were torn apart, ripped from the earth, as the natural distances between them were made into fields, as their root systems were unable to share the water that flowed beneath the earth.

Being trees, they did not weep, for they knew that man had come to the earth not long ago, and was very young. And ignorant. The trees knew that in parts of the world whole forests would be lost as man used them.

They also knew that in some parts of the world, certain people would discover their beauty, and work to save whole forests, but that the trees would be at the mercy of human beings till the Great Earth had to right the balance once again.

The trees had a secret that no other form of life on the planet contained. And this secret was to remain till the last tree was standing. Humans would not understand that trees could be guardians of property, could contain wisdom, could lead humans into the earth or up into the sky. Humans—at least most humans—would not understand the lessons of the trees, and the trees accepted this. Because one of their great secrets was they that knew the lessons they contained would rise again with the healing of the earth. The trees understood that, no matter how long it took for humans to understand that they had to learn to live on the planet as one of many life forms, equal but not superior, the trees would return.

THE
SHAMANS OF CHIRRIPO

While I was in Costa Rica, I was aided by several indigenous Shamans. I never met them face to face, but the messenger they sent to me told me how to enter their ceremonial place through deep meditation, describing the location and markings of the rock that served as an entryway to the cave-like place.

When I meditated with the crystal that was intended for this purpose, I could see the Shamans. They helped me know many things. They taught me when a shaman from San Jose or Peru was in the area to do dark work. They helped me to protect myself, showing me what objects I should hang outside my house to keep me safe.

They showed me when I needed to begin a healing,

encouraging me to wake up early, ride my horse, Chispa, into the valley, and ask for a sign from Creator regarding the healing. And they let me know when I needed to go into the forest to complete the healing afterward.

The Shamans introduced me to a group of small black birds that often appeared on the day I was to work with someone who was close to death. They showed me that the birds were a sign of illness and, depending on how they behaved, the person could be brought back from death's door, or they were meant to go on through. I worked with these birds often during the years I lived there, and they would always appear near my home on days I was doing intense healing work.

For the first two years in Costa Rica I would often feel a sudden push from behind that would make me fall. Although it could be amusing, it was not so much fun when I was walking close to the edge of a road that dropped off into a deep canyon below. The Shamans of Chirripo taught me that this was another shaman messing with me, and they showed me how to be more attentive and protect myself by stepping out of the way at the last moment.

They also helped me know when someone in the village was being attacked by a worker for the dark. This was important because sometimes people could get a bit paranoid and make up imaginary "enemies." However, some wealthy people in the area did bring shamans from Peru to mess with people's horses, businesses, or health. I could always rely on the Shamans of

Chirripo to tell me, through deep meditation, if there was truly a problem or not.

Finally, and maybe most importantly, the Shamans made me feel that I was not working alone. I was in a foreign country, and even though I learned the language, adding the layer of working in other realms was daunting. But the Shamans made me feel guided and aided. I am forever grateful to them.

In the years that followed, I did make three pilgrimages near the actual entryway to the Ceremonial site. Although, being non-native, I could not go onto the land, I left offerings, and I always expressed my gratitude.

But all of that came later. The first time I heard about them, I was taken completely by surprise.

FOUR STONES AND A CRYSTAL

One particular day, after several months in my Birthday Cake house, I looked out my window to see a large dark man, his shoulders much broader than most of the locals, walking quickly toward me. Oddly, he was coming through the woods, not from the dirt road that ran several hundred feet from the entrance to my house.

To my surprise, he spoke English. "A Shaman of Chirripo sent me," he announced as I opened the front door to welcome him.

"Excuse me, who sent you?" I asked, looking into sharp blue eyes, a startling contrast with his dusky skin.

"A Shaman of the Bribri tribe, of the mountain Chirripo." He was sweaty, obviously thirsty, and looked past me into the living room.

I invited him into my wooden haven.

The man stepped into the house and took in the rustic floorboards, some of which offered a view to the earth below. He sat in one of two rocking chairs carved of local wood. Taking his time, silent, he rocked. The floor creaked as always. I waited, comfortable with silence. This was a recently-learned skill for me, being comfortable in silence.

The sun from the Que Puta window shone into the living room where we sat. I offered him a cup of canella tea, which the man accepted. He wore the usual high rubber boots, brown tattered pants and work shirt, nondescript and male.

Finally he got down to business. "This Shaman at Chirripo sees you. Especially the younger son of the oldest one. They say you are a shaman and they need to know if you are the one they have been waiting for. He says you are the one if you can tell me about these stones."

From a pocket in his old pants, he produced four stones, holding them out in the palm of his weathered workman's hand. "Tell me which is from the North, East, South, and West. If you are correct, I will be back with gifts from the Shaman and his son."

I knew not to look at the stones. Placing one in the center of my left palm, I closed my eyes, and heard the North wind blowing through it and saw the light of the Northern skies.

"This is North." I handed him the stone.

I transferred another to my left hand, and White Buffalo Woman appeared to me. Although she is a Northern symbol, she appears to me in the South.

"This is South." He took the stone.

The third revealed the Light and Eagle of the East, and the forth, the depth and cave-like energy of the West.

He accepted the stones and my replies, nodding and making a mental note of my answers. He finished his tea and rose to leave. As he stepped off the porch, he raised his left hand in a goodbye. As I watched, he vanished like a deer into forest.

A month later the man returned. This time, he knocked once before opening the door himself. In his hands he carried a pig skin, a rattle, a huge chunk of crystal, and seed pods, gourds, and feathers.

"The shaman brings you these, and this note. He welcomes you and will help you. I translated instructions for you on the note. I don't remember what it says. Wrap the crystal in the pigskin for a couple of weeks while it gets used to your house. It's for your protection." He turned to leave.

"Wait." I gestured for him to sit. "Please. At least tell me how you know him."

"You got any more of that tea?"

I poured it into a cup from the kettle I kept hot on the woodstove and handed it to him.

"Be careful. It's hot."

It wasn't, but I had discovered that the local people never drank truly hot water, so I always warned them.

He sipped slowly, and sat back in the rocking chair. "I am Costa Rican. I have a child with a woman from their tribe. So I am now a part member of the tribe. I am no longer with her, but I go up there often to see my daughter. You can't go there because you are not dark skinned. No one goes there who isn't native. But they see you. They described you to me perfectly. They are the Bribri tribe, one that was not touched when the Spanish came. And one that, so far, the government has left alone. They usually have nothing to do with outsiders, so I don't know why they sent me to you, but they were very insistent. … Put that thing they made of seeds and gourds up like a mobile on your porch. And make sure to take care of that chunk of crystal. It's from the mountain. "

I stared at the crystal lying on the pigskin on my floorboards.

"How do you speak such good English?" I asked.

"I learned English in school and listened to the tourists in the city. I'm an artist. I need to speak as many languages as I can. To sell my work."

"Who are the Bribri people?" I asked.

"They are the only tribe left in the country who still follow the old ways. They refuse to be helped by the government because they don't want help. Poor. Very poor, economically. But rich otherwise. They are a people who know very little about today's world. That will change. It's good you are here now because I am sure that my little country, which is slowly becoming another star on your flag, will not tolerate their separateness much longer."

He paused. "Now, I have said more than I probably should, and although the tea is great, it's too hot for me. And I have to go. It's a long way home. "

As he began walking toward the woods, he turned and paused. "By the way, take good care of that crystal. You're going to need it," he said.

"Need what?" I said.

"Protection," he said. "I told you it was for protection."

And he was gone.

I sat back in my favorite rocking chair and thought about protection. Such a loaded word. I had learned well how to protect myself and yet the word always stirred something in my belly. As I pondered, I became aware of distant thunder and a darkening sky. I knew testing times were coming. But first I had to learn a few things from the animals.

SPIDERS IN
THE OUTHOUSE

When I first moved to Costa Rica, I lived in a cabin the rainforest, with a lot of holes in the walls and an outhouse out back. Lots of wildlife regularly entered the house: ants, beetles, flying beetles that would zoom right towards my third eye, tarantulas, snakes, iridescent bugs. It was a rainforest, after all. There was mold everywhere, and clouds often entered through the walls.

Patricia had taught me to honor all life forms. I remember once finding her in tears over the fact that she had unintentionally killed a small spider in her house by placing a dinner plate over it. She also taught me to try talking to animals if their lives and mine were clashing. She believed most, but not all, could understand.

The first time I went into the outhouse, I noticed two really large spiders tucked towards the back. I thought, "Hmmm. I wonder if they bite." Before I had time to really consider that, I noticed that they jumped—and they jumped long distances. And there they were, jumping around. I thought, "No way am I going in there." I slammed the door and went out into the cloud forest.

As the weather became colder, and the rains constant, I realized that I needed access to the outhouse. I took some Ajax and slowly opened the door. I didn't see the spiders, so I went in there and cleaned it thoroughly, thinking surely the spiders wouldn't return. The next day when I opened the outhouse door, there they were, back up in their corner. In the same position.

They were in the back of the outhouse, which meant that if I was sitting down, they could jump on me—all of a sudden—from behind. Scary thought. I remembered Patricia's advice. I began talking with them. "Look," I said, "this is my outhouse. You have the whole rainforest. Get out of here."

The next day when I opened the door, they had built a web across the doorway so that in order to get to the toilet seat, I had to break through their web. "Well," I said to them, wherever they were, "Very funny. Alright then. It's a war."

Since I couldn't see them, I was worried they were hiding below me, so sitting on the toilet seat was not an option. They won that day.

The next day I returned, and—I kid you not—they were sitting on the toilet seat. I slammed the door and went out into the rainforest. The following day, I opened the door and they were still sitting on the toilet seat. I said, "Look, we really have to come to some agreement. I live here. I have to use the bathroom.

Sometimes it's raining really hard. It's cold. Can't you two just go back up into the corner where you were to start with and live in peace? And I'll use the toilet seat and we will all just get along."

The next day the oddest thing happened. I opened the outhouse door and there they were, back in their original spot. I thought, "OK, if they jump on me and they bite me, I probably won't die. I will scream, that's for sure. And if I do die, it'll be one heck of an ending, someone finding me dead of spider bites in an outhouse in the rainforest." And I really did need the outhouse.

So I sat down. I used the outhouse. And from then on, the spiders stayed in their place, and I stayed in mine, and all was well.

THE ANTS
AND THE BELLBIRD

I came out of the house one day to find eight lines of leaf cutter ants heading to and from the Lauraceae tree in my yard. Each ant carried a tiny triangular bit of leaf from the tree, four lines marching to it, and four away. These ants can dismantle a tree in a day.

I love the leaf cutter ants. They carry their leaves like small sails. If one ant gets stuck, another comes along from behind and helps push through whatever the obstacle is in the pathway. The species is at least 50 million years old, and they improve nutrients on the rainforest floor. But they were headed to the Lauraceae tree that produces a tiny avocado, which is the only food for the highly endangered Bellbird. Because of lack of food and habitat, there are very few Bellbirds left.

I had spent hours collecting seeds as they fell from this tree and taking them to a nearby refuge, where people were working to grow more of these trees in order to save this unique bird. This particular tree was outside my bedroom window, and nearly thirty feet tall. On some lucky days, a Bellbird would land there, and let out its hauntingly beautiful call, a horn-like sound followed by three clear bell whistles that echoed throughout the rainforest.

There I stood, watching the ants dismantle the Lauraceae tree. What to do? Should I do nothing? Save the tree by killing the ants? Let the ants follow their ancient pathways and kill the tree? Let nature take its course? What was the course of nature? Why was I standing there in that position anyway? If I wasn't living there, it would all be in balance.

Once again, I thought back to Patricia. What would she say? I waited and waited. No clarity came as the lines of ants grew daily. Finally, I made a decision.

I decided to save the tree for the Bellbirds.

I put poison out for the ants, in the form of tiny pellets that the ants eat and take back to their nest. The pellets kill the whole colony.

I went into the house and put on James Brown and began dancing to take my mind off the dying ants. Three hours later I went outside and….sure enough, no leaf cutter ants. All quiet. Sitting there, I wondered, did I do the right thing? What was the right thing? There were a few leaf cutter ant corpses around. I covered them with dirt.

The next morning a Bellbird landed in the tree outside my window and I heard that long clear sound, echoed by three whistles that resounded throughout the rainforest.

Had I done the right thing? I don't know. I will never know.

THE INCH WORM

Over the years, I had dug up plants from the rainforest that seemed agreeable to being transplanted. My entire yard became a garden that needed only minimum care, with stone pathways running through it like a winding brook of rocks. The climate naturally provided enough sun, cloud cover and moisture, and since all the plants were from the forest, they followed their own blooming and dormant times. The tropical plants drew hummingbirds, butterflies, snakes—all manner of life.

My great morning pleasure was to sit on my woven hammock

chair, usually in my pajamas, drinking coffee and watching the garden. Every now and then something would catch my attention, and then I wouldn't return to the house for hours.

One warm dry day in February, I noticed an unusually bright green movement among the plants. I went to investigate and found the most beautiful, delicately-shaped inch worm making its way along one of the plant stems to the ground. First the front, then the back, first the front, then the back, making a horseshoe shape, and then lying flat.

How, I wondered, was such a creature possible? Tiny legs, so perfectly segmented, and so determined.

Over the next few hours, I followed this creature's journey across the garden. Being only about an inch long, it could not go faster than its body allowed, which was, by human standards, painstakingly slow. Yet it made progress. It didn't stop to eat much, although now and then it would pause on a leaf and absorb water from a dew drop. Its color, so deeply, improbably lime green, really stood out, and yet nothing attacked it.

I was hypnotized by its movement. It seldom paused, and seemed locked into its rhythm. Push up, straighten out. Push up, straighten out. I was fascinated as to what the destination might be.

I know very little about inch worms, but here was this tiny creature, fully knowing what to do, following some ancient DNA pathway that was its life, undeterred by small piles of dirt or odd shapes. It never lost its balance, never fell off a plant, just chugged along like the little engine that could. Proportionally, a human would have been traversing a forest of gigantic obstacles throughout the day.

My whole world was focused on that inch worm. Time passed as I followed its non-linear journey through the garden. Although many times I had an urge to touch it, I didn't. I thought the disturbance might make it curl up, or that it would somehow unhinge its rhythm.

Those entranced hours were like jewels to me. They reminded me of the first time I had, with Patricia's instructions, watched lizards for days in the Columbia River Gorge as they appeared as my first Power Animal.

Although I knew perfectly well that I was just watching an inch worm, still, wisdom came bubbling up: Don't be in such a hurry. You can only go as fast as your body allows. Go where you know to go. Rest when you need to rest. If you just concentrate on the next step, anything is possible. It was tiny but part of the whole, and it knew what it was doing; it knew its place in the great web of life. It took one thing at a time.

To this day, I often see the inch worm in all his glory, making its way across the garden, destination unknown.

TAMING MY HORSE

When I first decided to buy a horse, I asked around and a friend told me about a spirited pony at a farm nearby. I waited till I was confident that I could handle the deal in Spanish and not make any major blunders.

I called the farmer, and made a time to meet with him and see the mare. The day arrived and, dressed in old jeans, a work shirt, and hat, I started down the dusty road, hoping to give the correct impression of a gringa without a lot of money. Most locals assumed that all gringos were rich, and prices for everything from mangos to houses tripled. In the year that I had lived in the cloud forest, I had made some headway dispelling this belief, by living in the birthday cake house, and living as the locals lived. I had been told a few times that I was "mas Tica que Tica," an expression meaning literally "more Tico than Tico"…or "one of us."

On the hottest, dustiest days of the cloud forest dry season, you had to breathe through a cloth bandana. This was one such day, and as I walked, swirls of dust surrounded me. The sun penetrated my clothing and soon I was sweat-covered and dusty.

The farmer was waiting for me, as he said he would be. That in and of itself was nothing short of miraculous, since being on time was not a Tico trait: "on time" could mean anything from an hour to a day late. His name was Adam, and his life as a farmer was deeply etched in the lines on his face crossing every which way, like a map of trails through a complex landscape. His grey eyes were watery with the dust. He stood leaning against the wood gate, careful not to touch the barbed wire fencing.

Two horses stood head to butt, both covered with ticks. Neither seemed bothered by that, but both tails swished over the other's back to keep the flies at bay. The chestnut mare, a modest size at less than 15 hands, raised her head to reveal the blaze on her forehead. Her eyes signaled slight fear and a good deal of wariness.

In the up-and-down motion of the mare's head was a territorial challenge.

"How much do you want for her?"

"Two hundred. Two hundred American dollars." The slight farmer was so thin he looked like he might break. I knew I should bargain, but I didn't have the heart. He looked so worked, weathered, and just plain old that I couldn't.

He looked down at the toe of his boot, tracing circles in the dirt.

"Look, you should know this horse threw two other men who tried to train her. They both said she was que puta." (what a whore)

"I like her," I said. "She doesn't look like que puta to me. She looks like a sturdy, stubborn mare."

He smiled, "Well, stubborn, that's for sure."

"How old is she?"

"Five. She was just left to be with her buddy here for the first three years. Then one man tried to break her in, but he got so disgusted he brought her back. And then a year later, another man bought her but he wanted his money back. She's nothing but trouble."

"Well, I like her. I'll buy her, and arrange to come pick her up tomorrow."

"You sure? You got experience with horses?"

"Enough," I said.

He looked at me with doubt in his eyes.

"Because I don't want to see you coming back this way wanting me to take her again. You buy her, she's yours."

"Sounds good to me. It's a deal."

I shook his hand, and turned back to the pony. "You are coming home with me tomorrow. So get ready."

I had always wanted my own horse. By the age of 10 I was competing in horse jumping shows. All the accoutrements of English riding filled my closet; the pants that ballooned out at the thighs, the short sassy whip which I hated, my round velvet hat that made me feel like I belonged in an English hunting painting, and the well-cared-for boots. I loved the smooth, black glare of the boots. They fit perfectly and added three inches to my 4'11" frame. The riding jacket hid the fact that my chest was still perfectly flat. At age 12, I showed no signs of becoming anything other than a no-breasted short girl. The walls of my bedroom were filled with ribbons, shiny pink and red with little gold centers engraved with First or Second Place. Small fake gold trophies of women on horses covered the board shelves in my room, separated by plastic horse statues of every breed, size, and color.

My father refused to buy me a horse. No number of First Place wins would add up to my own horse. Too expensive to keep, he said. It made no sense to me, as the lessons, shows, and finding good horses to jump cost a lot of money. I was sure my father didn't want me to enjoy myself that much. Or, more to the point, to be out of his control. He was the one to drive me to the riding stables, to approve of the horse, to choose my trainers.

All I wanted was a small barn behind our ample house and a horse of my own. I wanted to ride bareback, unconcerned about the placement of my ankles, the curve of my spine, the height of an upcoming jump. Although I loved riding, I was always afraid in my solar plexus, and I knew the horses sensed it. The discipline of posture, and the gaited ease of English riding never felt right to my body.

Once, at a lesson, I approached a jump and I, not the horse, shied away at the last second. The instructor screamed at me, as my father watched.

"Never do that again. Do you hear me, young lady? That is the way to untrain and ruin a perfectly capable animal. Never approach a jump and then turn away. What are you trying to do, destroy a great horse?"

He gestured from the ground with his whip as he yelled. I felt the tears coming on, but refused to let them fall. My father stood on the side, by the fence, shaking his head back and forth in disappointment.

Later I would hear about it at home. All my life, at some totally unpredictable moment—as if an unseen signal had been given from above— my father would rage at me. Often he cornered me in the hallway, blasting me with words so loud I felt them go through my skin. Trapped in the corner, I would shake until, again with some hidden signal that I could not decipher, he released me from his outrage. I would flee into the bathroom, my refuge, lock the door, and stay in there, sobbing. Sometimes I stayed for hours even after the crying stopped, just to be somewhere quiet, out of his range. No amount of knocking on the door or encouragement from my mother could compare with the silence of the bathroom. Besides, there was a window above the bathtub, a possible escape route. I often imagined climbing out of it. Running away.

Now, in Costa Rica, purchasing my first horse nearly 45 years later, I was thrilled. No one to watch. No one to judge. No one to tell me what to do.

Although I had never trained a horse, I was sure I could. I began by asking the owners of my rented house if I could fence in a few acres for the horse, and they agreed. I named my mare

Chispa, Spanish for "a spark."

For days, I sat on a rock in the grassy fields observing Chispa as the mare trotted around her new surroundings. She would rub her back on a tree, smell the bushes, gaze out over the landscape down the mountain valley. On impulse, she cantered along the trails carved by leaf cutter ants, kicking up dust in what appeared to be a solo frolic. Rarely, the horse would come close, but never close enough to be touched.

Chispa had several acres of bushy, lightly-treed cloud forest as her home, the field a grassy stage for all manner of tropical birds and insects. A shelter under the roof of an old farmhouse provided relief from the sun, rain, wind, and cold. Although horses are herd animals, Chispa was quick to discourage any company, whether dog, goat, or cat. The Spark preferred to be left alone.

Chispa often stood under the shade of an old pine tree. She seemed to have an agenda, and it consisted of standing in the shade, wandering off for water, and returning to stand in the shade.

Sitting and watching the mare was a pleasure. We developed a rhythmical relationship of sorts. If I walked towards Chispa, the horse would let me get within three feet before trotting off into the bush. Twenty minutes later, Chispa would calmly reappear. This dance continued for several days. Neither oats nor water could convince Chispa to come within touching distance.

One day, I was sitting on the rock and Chispa walked right

up to me. No reason. No sense to it. Just sauntered on up and stood there calmly while I placed a light, soft hand on Chispa's neck and gently stroked her.

This contact grew till Chispa allowed company on her walks around the mountaintop home. We walked side by side.

One day Chispa allowed a halter to be gently placed around her head, ears, and under her chin.

I began walking Chispa around the field and talking nonstop with her.

"I know you don't like to be ridden, but I am going to ride you and we will take it nice and slow and I'll start bareback, no saddle, and we will just take everything one step at a time. No hurry. But I am boss here. One of us has to be, so that would be me. Not that I won't listen to you and love you. I will. But I am boss. So what I say goes."

If nothing else, Chispa became accustomed to these one-sided chats. Now the horse came to greet me, knowing the oats in the bucket would be the reward. Days passed, weeks passed, and one day I decided it was time to take Chispa into a nearby round pen and begin training her.

Chispa stood in the pen with her butt facing me. This was not an auspicious position; in fact, it was downright disrespectful. In my right hand, I held a long training whip. I cracked the whip near Chispa, who didn't move. I yelled. Chispa didn't move. I cracked the whip in the other direction. Chispa stood, dancing with her hind feet like a circus horse.

"MOVE, goddamn it, Chispa! MOVE!"

Chispa would rather feel the sting of a whip than move. Stubborn. Que puta. "Come on Chispa. GO. MOVE!"

Chispa turned slowly to look at me. Obviously the mare was the one in control and she knew it.

"OK. You win. But only today. Tomorrow I am coming back, and I will have help."

Piccaracho drank enough guaro, a powerful mountain whiskey, to put most of his peers to shame. He was a hard worker, constructing houses by day, as well as doing all manner of road work on the mountaintops of Monteverde. He lived in a wooden wreck of a house with his wife who was always angry with him. Hence the drinking. Or maybe she was angry because he drank. He was something of a town joke because by sunset the whiskey would be running through his veins and he would come staggering down the dusty roads though the village.

But he knew horses, and he was an excellent trainer. Many of the locals showed him no respect because he was poor and refused to work for the gringos, dress in clean clothes, and play the "Yes, Master" game to the wealthy Americans on the mountain. He preferred his whiskey, humble work, and being left alone. I liked him.

We had formed a bond when I had first bought the horse. He came to help me take the hundreds of ticks off Chispa, to wash the mare, and examine her hooves. He assured me that Chispa was a good mare, sound, could be trained, and had offered to help if I needed it.

Piccaracho was toothpick thin with a strength way beyond his weight. I had seen him lift heavy rocks and toss them like baseballs to help build a wall. He was also always willing to laugh. Every time we greeted one another it was like a celebration.

"AH! Como va?" he would ask with a smile that revealed large black gaps in his teeth. Eyebrows up in surprise and delight, arms wide open, he was childlike in his greetings. As one of the few Tico men who gave off nada in the way of sexual desire and actually understood the concept of a friendship with a female, he was a real gem.

With his help, Chispa began to move around the ring, and learned to trot, canter, and gallop when signaled. He helped me learn to put the horse through the paces, and every day I led Chispa to the round pen. I placed empty plastic bags around the ground so the mare would get used to them blowing in the wind.

Horses in Monteverde have to be trained well. The weather there could change swiftly. Not only that, all manner of vehicles made their way up the narrow dirt road. At 5,000 feet up, the potholed road up the mountain was for courageous drivers only. To stay safe, horses could not shy at Mack trucks, motorcycles, bags blowing in the wind, dogs rushing out to snap at their heels, screaming children playing in the middle of the road, or the occasional loose cow or bull.

I spent days walking Chispa into town, and standing on a corner with the mare while trucks, cars, cycles, buses, and stray dogs paraded by.

Then the day came when I decided to mount Chispa bareback.

"OK. Today is the day," I told the mare. "I told you when I got you that only one of us was boss, and that would be me. In spite of the fact that sometimes it's you. Today, it's my way."

I carefully pulled myself onto Chispa's back. We were in a field, far away from any noises and roads. I didn't want the horse to bolt, or rear up and throw me on anything harder than the ground.

Chispa, however, was perfectly calm and off we went in a gentle trot around the field. All was well. But I had not noticed the gathering clouds. Too intent on holding a gentle rein and watching for signs of anxiety in Chispa, I didn't see the approaching rainstorm.

The sudden loud clap of thunder shuddered through Chispa's body. Chispa reared up, ridding herself of the human nuisance on her back, and went running off into the field, the reins trailing at her side, the lead rope rustling along the ground as she fled.

The next bolt of lightning and smash of thunder sent her running further.

"Great. Just great," I thought, scrambling to my feet. "Well, I guess we both know who is boss, at least today. One for you, Chispa."

Finally the mare reappeared, her large, liquid eyes looking slightly curious. Maybe even a little sheepish. Soaked and shivering, the two of us walked home in the downpour, Chispa allowing herself to be led demurely by the lead rope back to her fields.

I went into the house for a hot shower and rest. In the background, thunder from across the valley still vibrated the house. I thought better of taking a shower, since I had what was known as a "suicide shower," some vague mess of wires that heated the water when I turned on the shower. I had been told never to use it when there was either thunder or lightning, and since the day lightning had blown out my TV, I paid attention to all such instructions from the locals.

Instead, I removed my wet clothing, hung it on the rope in a back room, and wrapped myself in a nice big warm towel. I sat in the rocking chair and listened to the light rain and felt the soothing rhythm of rocking back and forth. I glanced out the window. Chispa was calmly eating her hay, which was undercover and dry.

We were not that different, Chispa and I. We were content being alone. We were both stubborn and, in some ways, feral. I knew that love, patience, trust, and a firm hand would eventually tame her. And it did. I just had to do it my own way. And I think I knew, even then, how deeply healing the process was for me.

EAGLE FEATHER

One day I was riding the rickety local bus on the way back from San Jose, climbing the narrow dirt mountain road filled with potholes that led to Monteverde, when the bus came to a halt on the mountainside, nearly 4,000 feet up. I looked out and saw a line of local people staring over the edge of the cliff, talking loudly and shaking their heads.

I got off the bus along with everyone else. Even my imperfect Spanish allowed me to understand that a car had gone out of control during the night and veered off the narrow road and over the cliff. Two men were dead down there, but one was still alive. All the people were waiting for the Red Cross to arrive; they had been waiting for two hours. A farmer below sent word up that the man down there was probably dying.

For the past two weeks, night after night I had been dreaming that I turned into an eagle. In the dreams I began walking, then flying, as a creature that was part human and part eagle. In my daily meditations, I had been experiencing the same odd sensation of being part woman, part eagle. It would not have surprised me to open my eyes and see feathers on my arms.

Now, as I listened to the crowd of people, and looked up, I saw a pair of eagles flying in circles above the mountain valley.

Without thinking, and without hesitation, I began making

my way down the steep rainforest mountainside. I was wearing sandals, and I slipped on the dirt as I started my descent. My only thought was, "I hope I don't get chiggers."

The sun shone hot through the trees. As I stumbled down the mountainside, I was grateful that I had my water bottle and that it was full. I came upon bits and pieces of the car, a door crinkled like tin foil, another roof piece smashed against a rock, silver bundles of metal spread out through the bushes and trees, glaring in the sun.

I passed the first body, on his back, arms and legs spread. Someone had placed a red T-shirt over his face. He lay limp as a sack on the bare, dusty earth, as if that patch of land was especially for him.

I said a quiet prayer and continued, passing more metal pieces among the dirt and leaves of the forest ground. That first body was beginning to smell, and I covered my nose with my shirt sleeve. I continued down the slope, and passed the second body, this one contorted and a bit swollen, also covered with a T-shirt on the face, flies swarming all around.

I had seen death before, but not in this haphazard way. I had never seen bodies thrown from a vehicle and landing like garbage on a mountain.

I had no sense of how long I climbed down when I heard the moaning, and saw the man lying in a kind of ditch. He was on his back, groaning, a small dark-skinned man, surrounded by flies, his white shirt covered in dried blood and black pants wet with piss and dirt.

To my surprise there was a group of four men about 400 yards away, quietly talking. One was a policeman.

They said nothing to me, and I ignored them as I leaned over the man on the ground and began talking with him in Spanish.

He was somewhat coherent. He was thirsty. I gave him my water. His eyes hurt. I covered them with my sunglasses. He pointed to his arm, which was swollen and bent in an odd angle off to the left, still attached, but with bone poking through.

"Silencio," I said softly. Then I turned to the group of men. "Does anyone have a knife?" I asked.

They all silently shook their heads no.

"Will anyone help me get his shirt open?"

Again, all shook their heads once. No.

I had been living in Costa Rica three years now, long enough to know better than to try to convince a Tico man to help if he didn't want to. And long enough to speak Spanish and understand what the man on the ground was saying to me.

"Necessito ver a mis hijos, y mi familia otra vez. Si Dios me permite que puede verlos." My children, my family...I must see them again. Please God, that I may see them again.

I took hold of his shirt and ripped it open to reveal that half of his chest was crushed, and the other half had a hole about the size of a quarter in it. His breathing was difficult, and he suddenly became agitated and wanted to get up.

"I have to piss," he mumbled as he tried to move.

"No! No. Pee in your pants. There's no shame. You can't move. When you move, you hurt yourself. You have to be still. If you want to see your wife and children again, you have to lie still. Help is coming. I am sure. They are on the way. Just be still. Just pee here. I am not looking," I turned my head.

Flies were everywhere, on his chest, on my face, everywhere. I began spitting at them, and continued talking to him as the smell of urine combined with the stench of dried blood.

He was beginning to pass out just as I saw that the Red Cross had arrived and had managed to lower a canvas stretcher down the mountain. I gently touched his forehead.

"I see them. Stay awake. They are coming. I can see them at the top of the mountain. You must not go to sleep. Here, take a sip of water." I lifted his head slightly so he could drink.

I continued talking to him for another 30 minutes, till suddenly, there at my side, was a man in a Red Cross uniform. I told him what I knew, and immediately left and began the long uphill climb through the forest.

I had no water now, and it was past noon and hot. A farmer, who seemed to materialize out of the forest, walked in front of me, and began cutting a path through the brush with his machete. As he cut, he cursed.

"Qué gringa más tonta\ estúpida! Aquí no es para las mujeres. Qué mal. Muy malo. Estúpido." What a stupid woman.

Here is no place for a woman. Bad. Really bad. Stupid.

He cursed me as he cut the path, the whole two kilometers up the mountainside, till I reached the top. I paused there, and looked down into the valley. Just then two eagles flew directly overhead. They circled above me twice, then flew off into the blue.

I did not look at the crowd, but began walking quickly to the house of a friend who lived about a quarter of a mile up the road. There, on the couch, I collapsed, shaking, dehydrated, and weak. I drank glass after glass of juice. I took a shower, sobbing into the stream of cool water. That calmed me, and wearing my friend's clean clothing, she drove me to my tiny colorful Birthday Cake house.

I was shaken up, not by the dead men, and not by the man who was fighting for his life, but by the group of men who did nothing to help. I could not understand it.

I fell into a deep sleep, but the group of men intruded in my dreams. I dreamed of turning into an eagle, seeing the whole event from an eagle's point of view...the car careening off the cliff, bodies flying out, spirits rising into the sky, the struggle of the live man. I dreamed my journey down the mountain and back up. I awoke with a sense of wings on my shoulders.

I knew I needed answers.

The next day, the story was all over the town. I asked five different locals why the policeman and others would not help. All gave different answers: maybe the laws said they could not touch the man; there had never been a dead person down there before...maybe they didn't know what to do; maybe they were afraid of him; perhaps they didn't want to help because he was from Nicaragua; who knew...

The next evening on the news, I saw that the man was in a hospital, recovering, and talking about how he would not drink alcohol again because he realized how much he loved his wife and children and he never wanted to be stupid again, and how thankful he was for being alive.

During the next couple of weeks, I returned to the spot on the mountainside where I had begun my climb down, now marked with a large rock. I could not imagine how I got down that mountainside. Perhaps I had flown.

In a dream a few nights later, my teacher, Patricia, appeared and said only, "They were doing the best they could. Let it go."

In the morning, I woke up for the first time in days with a sense of peace. OK. So be it. I made myself a cup of coffee and went out to my porch to sit in my hammock seat and watch the morning butterflies and hummingbirds arrive.

There on my porch was a large eagle feather.

THE CAT WITH
THE BROKEN BACK

In Costa Rica, I had a reputation as someone who cared about animals. In rural Monteverde, people were often so poor that unless a cat or a dog had potential as a working animal, it got tossed over the mountainside or left in the middle of a road in hopes that it would be run over.

The longer I lived there, the more often people would leave puppies and kittens on my doorstep because they knew I would either adopt them or find them homes. One day I saw a car stop outside my gate. A man opened the car door, placed a cat on the gravel, and drove away. As I approached the cat, I saw that its back was broken. The most awful moaning came from its throat. I went inside, got a box, put the cat in it, and brought the cat into the house. This was on a Sunday, and the vets in the area were unreachable.

I knew my neighbor would come over and hit the cat on the head with a rock to kill it, but I couldn't bring myself to call him. The cat was in horrible pain, and that's a hard thing to bear…an animal in pain. I decided to walk to the nearest market and buy rum. Returning, I managed to grab the cat right behind the head, tilt it back, and pour rum down its throat. I thought that way the cat would feel less pain.

That whole night the cat moaned and cried, no matter how much rum I gave it. I sat up all night trying my best to practice a form of meditation where you breathe in the pain and breathe out something to ease it.

For the life of me, I don't know what kept that cat going. In the morning, I called the vet and asked him to come over and put the cat to sleep with an injection. He did, and we buried the poor animal out back. I asked him to teach me how to give the injection so that terrible experience would never be repeated. He left a needle and medicine with me.

Some months later, I told this story in a workshop. A women became very upset with me. "You mean you sent that poor animal to its death drunk?" She was horrified. A man said, "You should have let that cat die by itself in the road."

I thought about those two comments. Then I remembered the voice of my teacher. She would say to me, "Do the best you can, call it good, and go to bed."

Do your best. Call it good. And go to bed.

FALLEN TREE

The old growth trees in the cloud forests of Monteverde are giants, unlike any trees I had ever seen. Not only are they huge, but they house so much life. Myriad forms of bromeliads live in them, so that each one is a glorious testament to the push towards life, abundance, and diverse growth. The trees not only create a canopy of life in the forest, they also determine what will grow in their shady skirts. The forest floor is defined by the amount of light, creating plants which are able to proliferate in shade. The complex, interwoven greenery is almost too much for the eye to take in.

Even after living in the cloud forest for two years, each time I would venture to the Reserve to visit the Old Grandmothers, which is what I had come to call these trees, their grandeur and strength never failed to both awe and uplift me.

One day, as I was crossing a bridge high up in the forest canopy, I heard a crackling sound. I turned to see one of these giants beginning to unearth itself and fall into the forest floor below. Everything became slow motion as a part of this cathedral of life uprooted, tumbled, and collapsed on layer upon layer of life. It fell to the earth with an enormous crashing sound that sent waves of silence in its wake throughout the forest. Clouds of earthy dust, like an echo after the sound, rose into the air.

I stood in shock. I had just witnessed the death of a tree that had more lifetime than I would ever know, and that was home to countless forms of life. A tree, like all the old growth trees, magnificent and stunning in its beauty. I became aware that somehow in my body, I had become so used to the trees that it had never occurred to me that one could fall. They seemed so rooted, as if they had eternally been there witnessing the passing of life, the calls of the quetzals and howler monkeys.

As I watched the earth slowly settle around the fallen tree below, I began crying as if I had witnessed a fatal accident. I stood on the bridge, shaken and saddened. I simply could not believe that one of these trees that appeared so strong, so full of life, could suddenly collapse.

Then it slowly came to me that I had witnessed the end of one very long process and the beginning of another. That the tree had been rotting for many years, the earth too wet to hold even those giant roots, and that what I had seen was not something tragic, but part of the natural order of the forest.

Still I wondered: what would happen to all those flowers and bugs and birds that made that tree their home? What would become of the undergrowth, now entwined in bark and wood? What had been crushed in the impact? I would never know the answers. A lot of questions and no answers.

Although I had thought I was learning the lesson of constant transformation through the days of mist and fog, abrupt clearings, and nights of downpours and thunder, I realized that I still held to this childlike belief that whatever was present would always be there. I wondered where that thought, that belief had come from, so contrary to the ways of nature and anything I witnessed in the forest even as a child.

I don't remember learning this defense against life, this notion that everything would always last. But on some level, in spite of the deaths of people very dear to me, I had never really grasped impermanence. Now, watching that tree fall, I understood the inevitability of change. In my bones, I knew too that the appearance of great strength was not a guarantee that such strength was infinite. That within the appearance of strength, there may be fragility.

As I left the bridge that day, I was both grateful and sad to have witnessed the falling of the tree. With it, another illusion was gone.

A FLOCK OF BIRDS

Groups of small black birds began to appear around my Costa Rican house on days when I was going to have a significant healing session, meaning working with someone gravely ill, perhaps dying. The birds came in flocks of sixty or more, and settled in the trees around my house, silent, but present.

The morning I prepared to ride into the hospital in San Jose to see Maria's sister, I woke before dawn, saddled Chispa, and rode off to a place where I prayed and asked for help in my work.

Maria, a dear friend, had already lost her mother and cousin, and now her sister lay suddenly ill in the public hospital, unconscious and in pain that was eluding the doctors' efforts to find its cause. Maria had asked me to come and see what was happening with her sister, and I agreed.

As I completed my morning prayers for good work that day, I mounted Chispa and sat looking over the impossibly beautiful folds of mountainside rainforest off in the distance. Sometimes I could not fathom how I had been so blessed to live in surroundings teeming with so many wondrous forms of life.

Suddenly, the air filled with small black birds that settled around me in the treetops. So many flocked there that it looked as if an artist had colored the tree tops black as an afterthought.

Chispa did not like these birds; she didn't like any surprises in the air. She startled and began bobbing her head up and down, up and down, her signal that she wanted out of there. Home we rode, and Chispa was relieved to be unsaddled and free to munch her oats out in the pasture.

Maria pulled up in her car a couple of hours later, and off we went down the mountain to the hospital. It was called The

National Children's Hospital, although the clients were all ages.

As we entered the room where Maria's sister lay, I was struck by the lack of privacy. Six patients lay in the room, all in varying degrees of illness and pain, with no boundaries or curtains, no privacy for either them or their families. Some were on their knees at bedsides praying for their loved ones, others staring blankly out the windows of the tall building. As this was customary, everyone seemed comfortable with the lack of privacy.

I sat by the sister's bed. A small woman, unconscious, but making sounds as if her abdomen hurt. Hot forehead. Tiny hands. Anna. Lying there, so thin she was lost beneath the sheet, which was covered in sweat.

I lifted Anna's hand to hold it in my own and closed my eyes.

Slowly the pictures formed, like a slow-motion movie, but three-dimensional and filled with sounds, smells, tastes, and touch. Anna was five years old. Her mother was dressing her in a beautiful blue dress that had layers of lace forming ruffles. Patent leather Mary Jane shoes on her small feet. Her mother was preparing to walk Anna over a rainbow where many relatives awaited her arrival.

Anna thought she was going to church, and was happy and proud of her dress.

"A dónde vamos?" she asked in her small, quiet voice.

"A la iglesia," replied her mother. We are going to church.

"Qué linda!" said Anna, excited and willing.

"Vamos, chiquita."

Her mother started to walk Anna towards the bridge, but Anna paused.

"Un momentito, mami. No estoy lista. Necesito recordar." Wait a moment, I am not ready. I need to remember.

"Que, mi amor? Que necessitas recordar?" What my love, what do you need to remember?

"Solomente no hay prisa," said the child. "Estoy muy cansada, mami. No estoy lista. Casi." There is no hurry, I am very tired. I am not ready. Almost.

They stood there, looking at the bridge. The child rested against the body of her mother.

"Cuando estoy lista, puedes cargarme, por favor." When I am ready, can you carry me, please.

"Ah, mi amor, sí, sí. Esperemos. Todo está bien," replied her mother. Yes, my love, of course. Let's wait a bit. Everything is fine.

I opened my eyes and looked at the woman lying beside me. Anna was not coming back. She was almost at the threshold of death. She was gathering strength to cross over and her mother had come to get her.

Suddenly I noticed the blackbirds on the window sill of the hospital, at least eighty of them flying about and landing on the window. Anna moved beneath the sheet, groaning.

Maria asked me what was happening.

"I am so sorry, Maria, she is dying. So sorry. Do you want

to be alone with her?"

"Yes, are you sure?"

"Yes, I am sure."

"Shall I say goodbye?"

"Yes, tell her how much you love her and say goodbye and let her go. I am so sorry, Maria."

I waited outside in the depressing hallway with its institutional brown walls, people lined up in wheel chairs, on gurneys, a wall of pain.

Maria came out some time later, and in silence we walked to the car and drove the four hours back up the mountain. There is a way that Costa Rican women are at home in silence. They often escape into it for refuge, from their husbands, from their loneliness. And from death.

Back at home, I saddled up Chispa to return at sunset to the same spot and give thanks for the day. As we rode, I passed neighbors who shouted "Ooppèe!" a typical greeting as I rode by. I had earned a nickname on the mountain, la llegua....the mare. It was not an insult, but rather respect from the Ticos, knowing that I had trained this horse, and it expressed their joy at seeing me ride, as they did, from one place to another.

I came to the viewpoint and paused. The birds were there in the trees. The small black birds. Waiting.

I closed my eyes as the sun was just about to drop behind the horizon line.

The little girl signaled to her mother that it was time. Her mother picked her up in her arms, and slowly approached the rainbow bridge. Many gathered on the other side, and they disappeared into the whiteness of vague forms on the other side.

The birds lifted themselves from the trees and flew away, far away, off into the valley of the mountains, away from me and Chispa, away from death.

OWL WARNING

Every night for two weeks, an owl hooted near the window of my tiny house. I had never heard such a loud hoot—it alerted the entire rainforest. On moonlit nights I could see that this owl was huge. It perched high in a tree near my kitchen, but the sound was so loud it might have been right outside my bedroom.

One day, Nani, my friend and nearest neighbor, came to say this owl was bothering her, that she had a bad feeling about it. Nani, who often knew things, thought the owl was a messenger of no good.

The murders ripped through the innocence of Monteverde like a knife through silk, changing the inner and outer landscape of the place forever. It was the worst crime in Costa Rica's history.

I was riding home on my horse Chispa when the first helicopter appeared, headed directly toward the town, the chopping sound disturbing the usually peaceful mountaintop air. Chispa startled at the sound, and raced toward the safety of home, taking refuge under the barn roof. Helicopters never flew into Monteverde: the valley with its shifting winds was too dangerous, and the 5000-foot altitude was too high to safely make a passage through the rainforest for landing.

Then Nani came up the road, crying. Nani never cried, no matter what horrible things were said or done. She had a good, big heart, but she had learned to be tough, as life on the mountain sometimes held cruel surprises. But this day she came crying, and asked to come in.

Nani, short with deep almost-black eyes, was my dearest friend on the mountain. We were like sisters, walking together every morning, having coffee together nearly every day. It was Nani who had taught me to cook, take care of my garden, and shop. Nani was also as silly as I, and the two of us giggled and laughed easily. But this day Nani's tears flowed into her tea. Two Nicaraguan men had robbed the bank and taken 12 local people hostage. They were trapped in there, in the bank, unable to leave. Already three shots had been fired, and rumor had it that three people had been killed in the first hour. The ongoing siege was on the news, and we turned on the TV to watch.

As the drama unfolded, Monteverde was besieged by the

media, both local and national, descending like vultures, and Monteverde was filled with armed police, trucks, cameras, and strangers.

One of the robbers lay dead outside the bank steps, perhaps shot by a local policeman. The locals were told to stay in their houses; most of the town was cordoned off, so the people were forced to watch from a few blocks away. It was like watching a show from another planet. They witnessed a few of the hostages escape through a window in the rear of the bank and run for their lives into the surrounding forest. All through the night the whole town was paralyzed.

No one knew who was alive, who was in the bank. Frantic calls were made house to house, till word got out. William the mailman was in the bank. The florist. More shots during the night. The next morning, one of the bankers convinced the robber to come out, hands up, and that's when everyone learned of the nine dead people in the bank. They were all people known by everyone on the mountain. Good people, kind ones who had simply been in the bank to take care of their financial affairs. And now they were dead.

The town was in shock. Once the media and police thinned out, people stood in the town center day after day, through night-time candlelit vigils, whispering. Many were simply frozen, showing no emotion. How could it be? How could this have happened?

The government sent counselors who held meetings for anyone to attend. People began to unfreeze, and the tears flowed. A memorial of poetry, dolls, flowers, balloons, prayers, stuffed animals, written memories covered the entire downtown. Every day new prayers, more poetry. Huge black ribbons appeared on doorways as people tried to get back to daily life—but they couldn't.

Then the funerals began, funeral after funeral, pierced by the calling of the birds, the occasional rumble of thunder, all of us standing numbly beside grave after grave.

Monteverde was a small enough community that the absence of even one person was noticeable. Suddenly there were nine people gone.

Three weeks after the event, I was riding Chispa home when I suddenly felt I must go into the bank and clear out the energy. I had a strong feeling that some of those who had been shot still did not understand they were dead, and needed an explanation. But the town was very Catholic and I did not want to offend the priest. Then I heard my beloved teacher's voice in my head, as clear as though she was right beside me, riding next to me: "Go in and ask the bank manager."

I tied Chispa to a post outside the bank and entered. It was nearly closing time. I asked to speak to the manager, and was granted permission to enter his office. He indicated I should sit in the chair opposite him. He was a small man with an ample stomach, his shirt buttons nearly popping. He had kind eyes, and he looked at me with curiosity. We had done business for four years now and he knew me to be a trusted client in the community.

"Con permiso, tengo una pregunta un poquito differentè." With permission, I have a question....it's a little unusual.

He gestured for me to continue. I explained that I was able to do the work of a curandera, that I could clear the energy in the bank so that it would be lighter and easier for the people to work there and for the people in the town. I explained that everything I did would be in harmony with the church, that I could do the work with others present, maybe around closing time. I mentioned I might be singing, lighting a candle and some sage, walking around. And then I waited.

He answered immediately, and his response surprised me.

His eyes filled with tears and he said he would be so grateful. That they could hardly breathe in there. That working was nearly impossible. When could I come to do the work?

"In three days," I answered. "I will come in three days, at 5:00pm. And I am most grateful."

"No, it is I, it is we who are grateful. Just come in, and all but a few will be done for the day. Thank you so much for offering this to us."

I was startled at his manner, at how grateful he was; it was as though he had been waiting for someone to ask. As I rode Chispa back to my house, I began to see what must be done.

My teacher had taught me how to enter the World of Spirits, the world that had spontaneously opened to me as a child, and often irritated and sometimes haunted me as a young adult. Now I had the tools to shut it down or open it, and open it I did.

I contacted a group of ten people on the mountain, both locals and expatriates, who practiced a form of Japanese healing similar to Reiki. I asked them to gather in a house to the north of the bank on the date I was going there, and they agreed. I asked them to send light.

Then I approached a group of Quakers who lived on the mountain, and asked them if they would gather in a room down the street from the bank, and be still and pray for those who had been killed. They agreed.

I called healers from North America and asked them to drum at the time I would be in the bank, and they agreed.

Most importantly, the shamans of Mt. Chirripo had taught me how to enter, through deep meditation, their sacred healing space, and to ask for their help. I did this through a specific ritual, and they agreed to assist me.

Essentially I had the four directions covered, groups and individuals holding protection and sending light from all four directions.

Then I began my research on the history of the bank. I was not surprised to find that in the past, on the same ground, there had been a bar, and that there was violence and death associated with that bar. Before the bar, there had been a house, where a child burned to death. The ground itself had a history of violence and death.

I asked all those involved not to speak about the cleansing, that for their protection and mine it was best kept quiet. Also, I did not want to be known for this work, as it was not me, but the combination of everyone, that would make the bank clear.

On the evening I entered the bank, I had prepared with rituals of protection for myself and everyone involved.

When I walked in, I could see five bodies lying in pools of blood on the floor. Undead. This type of "seeing" was something I was born with, and I was not surprised at the bodies; I knew they were spirits. Unsettled. Not understanding. Shocked. Still not able to go.

I sat among them, vaguely aware of the three people left working in the bank, who purposely ignored me. I knew I had to work in a way that would not alarm or offend the workers.

Quietly I began by lighting a candle and clearing the space with a small bit of sage and juniper. I brought a large eagle feather to send the energy out and up into the sky where it could be transformed into light.

I began explaining to the five souls what had happened to them. How the robbers had entered, through what door, and to each I explained that they had been shot, and that they were dead, and could go home to their god now. In fact, I told them, they must. So that life could go on. Their relatives were saying goodbye, they were, in fact, now buried in the ground, so they would not be able to re-enter their bodies. They had to go. It was done. It was okay. They could go in peace. Their families knew they were dead. They must not stay there. Here. Here was a good light to look into. Watch. There were angels coming, relatives who were already on the other side. They were to watch them as the dead came to greet them.

Slowly, one by one, they left, going into the light.

I placed a small statue of Mary in front of me. I sat still till I could see the light begin to emanate from the center of the room and slowly spread inside the building, into every crevice, every darkened space, into the earth, deep, and now circling the bank on the outside, like a small hurricane of light. Then into the sky, into the nighttime, signaling to the stars that all was well on this tiny spot of earth, that the spirits were at peace, had gone home, and It Was Done.

I rose slowly after a long prayer of gratitude and closed the work. I did not know that several hours had passed, and as I rose to leave, I noticed that only the bank manager was left, waiting for me.

He was crying.

Without words, I hugged him and left, walking down the street to the room where the people were gathered at the end of the street. I entered the small, dark room, and asked them what they had seen.

"Light," they said. "Light first coming from inside and then swirling around the outside of the bank and into the sky."

I thanked them and said it was done. I felt faint, and one of them offered me a ride home.

After I entered my house, I began vomiting, again and again. Then, spent, I walked out into the night and listened to the night sounds. An occasional dove call or mot mot. Mostly crickets, in chorus with tree frogs.

I slept for a day and a night.

A week later, when I entered the bank, I was delighted. The priest had brought a beautiful statue of Mother Mary to grace the corner of the bank. Large plants stood in the other corners. Local artists had hung gorgeous paintings on the bank walls. Behind each teller's window, they now had tiny personal belongings, pictures of their families.

It was done.

The owl was silent, gone. I never heard that particular sound again.

SEEING
WITH THE FEET

I walked through the Children's Eternal Rainforest in Monteverde, Costa Rica, under a full moon. I moved without a flashlight, using my feet as eyes. For many years I had wanted to befriend the night, but until I met a Costa Rican forest guide, I had been held back by fears of the darkness.

He had grown up in the forest, and loved the land. To him the forest was a second skin. He taught me how to walk through the forest at night, even with no moon, using only my feet and breath to guide me. Over many weeks' time, I grew comfortable by myself in this dark other world.

In the Costa Rican rainforest, there were many unexpected sources of light: glow worms glided gently along the forest floor, mushrooms glowed a purplish color in the dark, leaves took on an iridescent quality, lightning bugs and other insects blinked on and off as they crawled along the ground. Although these light beings were tiny, their brightness was a welcome bit of glow now and then.

The full moon illuminated the cloud forest with a soft light that made walking less of a physical challenge and more of a psychic experience. I began to feel the presence of an animal before it moved. I could tell when a bird or a snake was nearby, my body feeling specific sensations: a tingling in my ankles that warned me of snakes, a softness in my chest that meant bird.

Walking at night was like walking into one's own darkness and finding guidance there. When I began, the guide taught me the technical aspects of walking at night: how to step onto a fallen branch from a distance and step a good long step off in order to avoid disturbing snakes, how to calm my breath at the sight of a pair of gleaming eyes through the forest, how to be aware of the branches above me as well as below. How to listen and know that a large animal might be near by the utter silence and cues of the paw prints.

As I learned to walk on my own, these nights were some of the most precious of my time in that country. The slow melting of my fear allowed me to experience the magic of the forest at night, the rhythms, sounds, and energies. It was only different from the day. Not frightening, only different.

One night as I was walking slowly, under a tiny sliver of a moon, carefully staying in my feet to sense the downward slope of the trail I was following, I heard a whisper in my left ear. I paused to see if I would hear it again.

"We are dying." The words were clear, although not human-sounding.

"Who?" I asked mentally, not wanting to speak out and disturb the night sounds.

"We, the jaguars, are dying. Help us."

I paused, aware of the vast valley of rainforest below, the

soft upward air currents. I had seen this valley many times in the day, and watched butterflies float on the currents below, as well as hawks, vultures, and the occasional mist wafting through the valley.

The voice I was hearing was not exactly in words, but the message was clear, as though a translator was encoding it in sounds I would recognize.

"How?" I asked again silently.

"Make room. We need pathways. We want our forest back."

I stood in the dark, looking at the slight moon, tilted in the sky, the stars clear. Locating the North Star, I sat on a rock and drew my breath in and all my energy into the center of my being so I could be as compact as possible, invisible and quiet, simply another being in the forest. I listened intently. This is the story I heard.

"When we, the jaguars, are gone from this country, that will be the end. That will signal the last of the ancestors leaving, and the heart will be taken out of this earth. We carry that heart, the soul of this land, what you call the Middle Americas. But humans have destroyed so much of our territory we have not enough food, nor enough land to roam and raise our young. There are not many of us left. We have been hunted, starved out, and the humans do not know that we carry the oldest knowledge of these lands. Once we are lost, all will begin to die. The humans love to think of our strength, our beauty, but they do not honor our physical being. "

I sat and listened, as a small glowworm made its way across the rock. Tears were falling and I realized they were mine. Helpless. I felt helpless.

"I am not good at organizing. I don't know how to help. Please tell me what to do," I thought.

Silence. Then an owl hooted close by. I had taught myself not to startle, but to let the sounds flow through my body.

So much time passed that I thought whatever had spoken to me had given up. Then, suddenly, I heard the voice again, this time in my right ear, and very clearly.

"It is not a matter of doing something big. Take other people, one at a time, through the forest at night. So they can feel the beauty of it. The wonder of our home. This is our time, at night. Let them learn to walk with us. We will stay unseen. "

"I will do that. I promise I will."

"Ahhhh."

That was the end of the conversation. As I stood to walk, the owl hooted again. I felt suddenly overwhelmed with tiredness, and instead of continuing, lay back down on the rock, shaping my body to its hardness. I slept and did not wake till dawn.

In the following months, I took many people on night walks through the forests, always telling them somewhere along the way, usually at the end so as not to frighten them, that the jaguars too walked at night. That we were walking in their territory and that whatever interest they might have in helping to preserve the lives of these gorgeous and powerful beings would be appreciated.

I went to visit a center in the southern region of the country where work was being done to help the big cats survive. And another center where former poachers were taught and paid to guard the rainforest so their livelihood did not depend on hunting the jaguars. At last count, the jaguars were increasing in numbers, but they are still very vulnerable to the cutting of the forest lands. I have never forgotten my message from Jaguar, and now I offer it to you in hopes that this story will inspire you to take action on behalf of this beautiful creature. The Defenders of Wildlife site, for example, has a page devoted to jaguars, along with suggestions for things you can do.

BEFRIENDING THE WIND

I am enfolded in the mossy lap of a giant old growth tree in the Monteverde Cloud Forest. This particular tree is a friend of mine, way back in the forest and high enough to allow a view of the unfolding greens and rolling valleys below. The wind is whipping all around me; if I close my eyes, it sounds like a churning ocean.

I have, in fact, hauled myself up to the tree with the intention of befriending the wind. Every year in Monteverde, there are three weeks of strong winds, so strong that residents defer to paved roads instead of walking on the dirt, close to the edges where long falls into the valley below await on either side. So strong that peoples' faces shift during the second week, and no one sleeps well. The wind is cleansing, reshaping, blowing away the leaves, dust, whatever needs to be shifted, but it is relentless, day and night, lasting for up to a month. It cannot be shut out even inside the coziest room; there is no escaping the sound, the upheaval of dirt and falling of trees, the occasional near miss of an empty plastic carton blowing at eye level across a road. Every walk is a potential accident wanting to happen.

This wind is serious business. It is too much wind for most humans to bear, and many on the mountain seek lower ground till it has passed. The horses are nervous and cannot be still; horns honk to get people out of the road. The dogs that roam the towns and forests seem to be in a hurry, ears blown back as they seek the next shelter. Everything is in urgent motion. No respite.

In the midst of this atmosphere I have come to make peace with the wind, as it has been blowing through my restless dreams that have seemed unbalanced, slightly off kilter. I am dressed in waterproof pants, boots, and a very warm coat with several layers beneath it, as I know too that the wind blows right through to the bones. Even though the temperatures may range from the high 50s up, the wind feels cold and cuts into materials, enters the pores, and whistles through the bone marrow.

I have also brought a flashlight and enough food and water for 12 hours, not knowing how long this befriending will take. I am in it for the long haul, and will not leave till I have some sense of coming to peace with the wind. It has been calling to me. "You can't resist me," it says. "You are powerless to affect me," it says. "There is something in me for you, if you will only listen." It's this last message that has brought me to the tree I call Lap Tree. It is home to an abundance of bromeliads, hosting so many forms of life that its vitality is palpable as I sit in its lap. I am sheltered from the wind, though not from the sound. If I stick my head out, the wind hits me full force, so I sit back and arrange myself comfortably, making sure my food and water are secured.

Sitting directly on the damp roots, my back against the hollow of the tree, I relax and calm myself after the hike through the wind up to the tree. No one is in the forest because of the danger of falling trees, but I have been careful on my way up to listen and watch for giants that might be about to uproot themselves. I am grateful for whoever invented waterproof pants, for mine are the only reason I can sit comfortably. So bundled am I, that movement, a change of position requires forethought, and as I listen, I drift into an on-again off-again sleep, aware of the wind washing its way through both.

I can feel my heartbeat through the layers of clothing, and at some point I tuck my gloved hands under my armpits for warmth. On and on blows the wind, and there I stay, curled up like some snail in its tree shell. Ever so slowly I begin to hear tones in the wind. They are not one-noted, but more like the songs of the humpback whales, rising and dropping, being sent across the surface of the planet. The wind has voices. I am not surprised by this, only a bit perplexed that it has taken me so long to hear them. The tones are behind, or deep inside the rush of air that is on the surface, that ocean sound washing through our days and nights.

I sit up in my tree cave, fully alert now, and listening intently. Momentarily I notice the light has shifted away, a sign that I have been there several hours. Closing my eyes, I follow the tones. "We are sweeping away the memories, the darkness, the old sounds that are not needed here. We are singing the dust and debris away, letting the old ones return to rest here. We are clearing the talk and minds of visitors, of the hurried ones, cleansing the roots and all they support that the forest may lighten and be lean.

"We are bringing in the sounds of the old ones, the ancient ones who dwell here always, that the tree spirits may be safe and show themselves to the rare one who wants to see. Across the universe we sing the sorrow of the people, the lament of lost moments, the opening of creation.

"The people are upset. The wind is too much for them. We know. We know. But even mountains must be cleansed and what you see as trees blowing is one dance that the tree beings create each year at this time in response to our tones. It is a big letting go, a huge letting go, and the people are anxious because they are reminded that they can hold onto nothing. Not one thing, not even their lives. This wind makes humans unsettled, unsafe, challenged, stirred up. So be it."

I go into a dream, and see dogs, kittens, bits of clothing, skin being blown away, over the mountain, across the vast deserts, into the sky. I too am blown off the edge of the road and find myself in the midst of a tone, a low tone that is sweeping me along with old branches and dust. The wind is blowing straight through my body, cleaning out every thought, every bad memory, all the disease, every breath not fully taken, filling my lungs with clean chambers, opening my throat, and when I awake, not only am I warm, but I cannot bear to be hidden from the wind.

I step out into it. I open my coat, take off my hat, and, standing firmly against the tree, eyes closed, I sing with the wind. I sing its tones. I could be in some church down on my knees in prayer and gratitude, but I am where I belong, in the rainforest, singing my own hymn with my new and dear friend, the wind.

BUTTERFLY
IN THE STORM

After five years, I knew it was time to return to America. I had been visiting friends in the Valley below Monteverde to say goodbye, and I was climbing up the steep hillside from the San Louis valley on the way home to my Birthday Cake house, feeling anxious and miserable. Leaving Costa Rica was like tearing the roots of an old growth tree out of the earth; it felt like my insides were being ripped apart. I was plagued by the image of an old tree floating in the sky, its bare roots seeking ground in space and finding nothing. But my guides were insistent: my work here was done. Distracted by my own distress, I was startled by a sudden violent thunderstorm. Sheets of driving rain. Deafening thunder. Lightning striking so close I could smell the burning.

Head down, I continued to climb, clinging to the rocks with slippery wet hands. I began to cry and pray. Every time lightning struck nearby, I jumped and cursed myself for what might be my fatal thoughtlessness. I knew better. I knew from experience that being outside in this valley was dangerous; my body was a perfect landing place for the lightning that danced over the mountain tops and into the valley, seeking a target. I began to fear that I might never get to the house, that perhaps I would die. Maybe this was my last day on earth. "Goodbye Liam, goodbye Bob, goodbye Julie, goodbye Nina." I said goodbye to my loved ones as I continued climbing.

The storm was getting worse. Finally I found a large rock and squatted behind its base, hoping to hide from the lightning. I was weeping and soaked, shaking, scared and miserable. Battered by the rain, startled by every crash of thunder, I was brutally aware of being alone, small, just a little vulnerable life form on a big mountain. And I gave up. Fine. If this was my death, fine. Others had died from lightning on the mountain in the years I had lived there. Why not me? Not a bad way to go. Sudden. Death by light. OK. I shuddered. OK, so be it. "Goodbye Debby, goodbye Susan, goodbye George."

At that moment, against all odds, out of the chaotic winds a butterfly appeared and landed beside me, a yellow swallow-tailed butterfly. I stared as it calmly opened and closed its wings, sheltered by the rock.

Butterflies had followed me throughout my life, often appearing in times of danger. In fact, I have a morpho tattooed on my chest, just below my collarbone.

Before I left the States, my teacher Patricia had told me to let the butterfly know if I ever needed assistance, and she promised that she would always come. Most people think shape-shifting is a metaphor, but Patricia could actually appear in different forms. This butterfly was most definitely a visit from her.

Now as I watched the butterfly and focused on the opening

and closing of its wings, on the rhythm of it, like a heartbeat, my own heart slowed. Gradually the sounds of the storm receded from my consciousness, and I was aware only of the silent, steady opening and closing of wings. This delicate creature could survive these mountains. Looking at the lines on the wings, knowing they were dust that shone in sunlight, I grew very calm. "Dust in sunlight, we are dust in sunlight," I told myself. Then the butterfly disappeared, swept off by the winds into the canyon like a tiny heartbeat.

Gathering my strength, I began to climb again. The storm raged around me, but the energy in the air beside me had shifted. It was as though I moved within a protected bubble of calm, unafraid. My teacher had helped me. Perhaps the crystal from the Shaman of Chirripo, given to me five years earlier, had helped me, too.

Finally my Birthday Cake house came into view, and in a few moments I had opened the door and collapsed in tears among the suitcases, thinking, "What a fitting last day of my life in Monteverde." And so it was.

Five years earlier, when Patricia had told me the rainforest trees would be my next teachers, I thought she meant it literally, but I came to understand this wasn't what she meant. By living in the cloud forest, in a wooden house which let all manner of creatures in—bugs, spiders, tarantulas, zorros, rats, snails, scorpions—I came to find my place in the natural order of things.

The trees that surrounded my house, and the trees in the Monteverde Reserve, allowed me to feel deeply held by Mother Earth in a way I never had before and never have since.

It's hard to explain, but I felt safe and held. No matter how crazy life appeared at times, I knew the Mother was taking care of me. I could get my feet way down into the soil there, and I developed deep, deep roots. I did not feel separate from the forest. Whether I was there in torrential downpours, storms, winds, or on bright sunny days, I continually felt held in the lap of Mother Earth.

This was healing in a way that allowed me to heal others. The most horrible things were tolerable there because of this feeling of being held. I think this is what Patricia meant. She knew I had never experienced the relaxed body of a baby held in her mother's loving arms. But I was finally given that experience by the land in Costa Rica, and it changed me forever.

PART III

LIVING WITH THE
REINDEER PEOPLE

When I was a very young woman, before I had any idea that I was a healer, I carried a postcard in my wallet. Over the years, it grew creased and scratched, but it was a kind of talisman for me. I don't remember now where it came from, but it showed two Mongolian shamans in full regalia. I had always felt a pull toward Mongolia, so once again, all those decades ago, I was evidently being guided along my path by something bigger than me, something that knew I needed to go to Mongolia, to meet a descendent of the first shamans. It became a dream I yearned for with all my heart.

After I returned to the States from Costa Rica, I finally found the love of my life, Wil, who eventually became my husband. Together we made plans to visit the Reindeer People. To make my dream a reality.

JOURNEY TO
THE REINDEER PEOPLE

We crouched on a peak in the Altai Mountains, bracing against a storm that had swooped in, bringing stinging sleet along with operatic thunder and lightning. The horses who carried our gear stood tied to a tree and the herders gathered with the horses, huddled among them, muttering calming words to the nervous animals.

Wil and I had been riding toward the Reindeer People, the Tsatsaan, through the rough mountains and forests, across rivers, and over steep landscapes, terrain that these Mongolian horses crossed effortlessly. It was a ten- to twelve-hour ride to the summer camp of the Reindeer People, where I hoped to sit face to face with a woman shaman, a direct descendent of the first shamans on earth. It would be the culmination of a dream for me.

Now the sleet was turning to snow, and the winds were picking up. It was the first time I had ever seen lightning in a snowfall. I was cold and my spine ached. Our saddles were Mongolian, about the size of a small pillow, consisting only one layer of padding over wood. The stirrups were set high, and I was glad we had brought our own stirrup straps from the States that could be lengthened to fit our legs, but the back of the saddle had a metal loop that served as a backrest, and mine hit just above my tailbone. I could feel the oozing of painful blisters from the continual chafing. Wil looked pale and sick, dizzy and weakened from cold and lack of protein. While I was grateful that we had layers of the right gear to wear, still I wondered if we were going to die here.

The heavy sky poured its freezing burden down on us, sleet scoured our faces raw, and thunder deafened us just moments after lightning flashed. What if we were struck by lightning? We were up too high, vulnerable, without refuge. I began to pray. For the first time since the storm in Costa Rica, I felt really scared, my heart beating wildly.

But in just a few minutes the storm shifted, and the herders signaled we were to mount the horses and continue. Riding into a gentler sleet, we were all relieved to be moving.

At the top of the mountain ridge the view opened up, revealing grand snow-covered mountains and a green valley below. The rushing streams were behind us now, as were the tall, black-fly-infested forests that reminded me of scenes from Dr. Zhivago. We rode on, the steep muddy trail down the mountainside hard to negotiate. From time to time, I dismounted, stepping carefully alongside my horse. Below us, I could barely see the tiny dots of tipis on the valley floor, shining in the setting sun. I was relieved, thinking we would be there before dark.

But the trail down to the Tsataan camp was slow going. It was hours later, long after dark, that we stumbled from the horses into a tipi known as the Hotel, and lay on the damp ground. We were soaked. Everything was soaked. Our clothes, gear, everything. And cold. The floor of the tipi was uneven. And cold. Immediately the herders came in with wood and made a fire in the small rusty woodstove that stood at the center of the tipi. The herders began hanging our belongings and clothes on strips of cloth, crossing the tipi inside till the roof hung with a wet web of everything.

Wil and I lay on the ground, spent. Two members of the tribe brought us warm bread and cheese, and it took all our strength to sit up and thank them, and then more effort to chew. The women returned with warm reindeer milk to wash down the bread and cheese, and our bodies slowly thawed, the food and drink reviving us enough to reach for dry clothes wrapped in garbage bags deep inside one of the packs. Closing the tipi flap, we changed, and spread dry pads over the wet ground and then the warmed sleeping bags over the pads.

I was aware of bleeding blisters on my back, low on my spine, but too tired to do anything about them. I lay on my side with closed eyes, imagining the horses stepping back up the mountains.

Slowly, through the haze of fatigue, cold, and pain, I realized that many people had come and gone to make us warm, give us food—people who had next to nothing. People had welcomed us, children peeked in and giggled. The herders had tied the horses, hung our belongings above the fire.

As I gradually warmed, it began to sink in: I was finally here. Our twelve-hour horseback journey was over. And we were here—here, at last, after all the years of yearning, of longing to actually meet a woman shaman descended from the original shamans. Now I was sitting in a tipi among them. Overwhelmed with wonder, gratitude, and exhaustion, I lay down again and fell asleep immediately, too tired to dream.

Next morning, stepping out among the tipis and reindeer into the pre-dawn light, I oriented myself by the faint glow that was the promise of a rising sun. Everyone was asleep but the young reindeer, who had been tied down at night close to camp so the wolves wouldn't hunt them.

I looked at the taiga, the stream, the surrounding hills and tipis. Moving quietly so the dogs wouldn't bark, I walked to the stream and dipped in a hand to test the water. Cold. Very cold. Although it was June, there was a dusting of snow on the hills and a chill on my face as I walked back to my tipi.

Before coming here, I learned that this tribe had lived in northern Mongolia since the 1947 closing of the Russian/Mongolian border. Like that of so many hunter-gatherers, the culture and very existence of these nomadic people are threatened. Although the democratic reforms of the 1990s gave the tribes ownership of their herds once again, the herds are terribly depleted, since the people are forced to sell or barter the animals that are their only real currency.

Now I could see firsthand what daily life was like for them: it was a grinding series of daily chores necessary for bare survival. Fetch water. Boil water. Make bread. Clean tipi. Carry wood. Separate wood. Release the reindeer. Carve molted reindeer antlers for the tourists who would come to meet them at Lake Khovsgol Nuur. Mend clothing. Gather the reindeer. Milk them.

As I sat thinking about this, Zaya, a young Mongolian woman, entered our tipi. Zaya had been to the States where she had learned English. A few years ago, while visiting the Reindeer People and working with them through a Non-Governmental Organization, she had fallen in love and married one of the young men of the tribe. She lived among them, following the traditions of the women and serving as interpreter for tourists who arrived.

"How was your night?" Zaya asked. "Did you enjoy the Tipi Hotel?"

"Fine. We are fine," I answered.

"I don't mean to be rude," I said, "but I would really love to speak with the Shaman sometime today if possible. Would you be so kind as to ask her if she would speak with me?"

Zaya looked down at the ground, and chewed on a piece of bread. Her tough, stout frame dressed in western sweatshirt and pants made her look like a she-bear.

"The Shaman is shy. She doesn't like to talk with strangers. Sorry. I know you came a long way. But that's the way it is."

"I understand, but I think she might be willing. Would

you mind asking her later, when she has a moment? Is asking her possible?"

"I will ask. But don't expect much. I am going to get you some reindeer milk, and enough for your husband. We are glad you came, and later you can see the carvings the men make from the reindeer antlers. There will likely be something you might like to buy."

Zaya's manner was abrupt, the expression in her eyes almost stern. Possibly the arrival of more and more tourists to this remote area was a drain. It was obvious that the Tipi Hotel was a money-making venture, and I was sure the Tipi Hotel had been Zaya's idea. The only one to traverse the world of the Reindeer People and the outside world, the young Mongolian had knowledge that no one else in the tribe could imagine. Tourists would want to be in a tipi, not in a cramped tent. They would want a fire and warm bread. So give it to them and make them pay. Call it a hotel, and—voila! Money.

As the sun rose, camp life revealed its morning rhythms. Fires were lit in wood stoves. Reindeer were set loose to graze. Women came out of the tipis and made offerings of reindeer milk to the four directions. The dogs barked and were thrown scraps of food. The men set off up the mountainside to gather wood. It was a warm day, and many of the reindeer stayed in camp, circling the tipis to avoid the flies.

I walked a respectful distance away to lift my skirt, squat, and pee. To my dismay, a group of reindeer came running full speed towards me. I thought I was going to be trampled and, as I fell backwards, I managed a laugh at the thought of the headline: "Woman Killed while Peeing in Reindeer Camp." The reindeer came to a sudden halt, and waited for me to gather myself together and leave. It was the salt in the urine they were after. Future trips to pee went smoothly as I watched them approach and talked with them. "Hang on there, folks. Urine comin' right up. Just hold on to your antlers."

MEETING THE SHAMAN

Zaya appeared in our tipi a few hours later as we were munching some almonds and dried fruit we had brought from the States. Wil had made several forays along the river, exploring our immediate surroundings, and he had created order out of chaos in the Tipi Hotel.

Now Zaya parted the tent flaps.

"Sain Tsetseg says she will see you. She says she saw you coming and is happy to talk with you. I will interpret if you like, or you can go in by yourself."

"Please come. I would appreciate your help this first

meeting," I said. "When?"

"Now." Zaya led the way.

The two of us walked across the camp, the tiny grasses and weeds alternating with areas of bare dirt and dust. There were reindeer droppings everywhere. The elder women of the tribe watched as we approached the shaman's tipi, which was a bit removed from the others.

Zaya opened the flap and we stepped in. It was only just light enough to see. The smell of earth and pungent juniper filled the air. This was the smell of a shaman's world. I recognized it, and suddenly felt slightly disoriented, out of place and time, with a sense of being both in and out of my body at the same moment.

On a wooden bench, tending the fire, sat Sain Tsetseg. She was dressed in her dal, the traditional clothing of Mongolia, a thick silk robe that served to keep out both the heat and cold.

Her dal was a brilliant blue, the color of the silk ovoo, a great tree or long stick in the ground covered with blue silk cloths in honor of the sky, offerings to the Sky Spirits. Since the sky was worshiped throughout the country by both indigenous tribes and Mongolians, these ovoos could be found on any hillside. One was supposed to walk three times around an ovoo clockwise and give thanks.

In contrast to her sky-blue dal, Sain Tsetseg's eyes were small, dark, and warm, deeply sunken in her round face. The shaman gestured for Zaya to sit to her left, and for me to sit across. I had the feeling there were more people in the tipi than the three of us. The shaman's energy was very held within, as though her belly contained a personal fire made of glowing coals. As Zaya had said, she was indeed shy. She offered bread, and cups of reindeer milk. We sat in silence for a few heartbeats. Then I broke the silence.

"Please tell her I am grateful that she would see me."

Zaya translated, then replied. "Sain Tsetseg knows you to be a shaman, and is happy to meet you. She could see you coming up the mountain. You are welcome here."

I carefully reached for the tiny crystal I had brought with me across the ocean, through the mountains and forests, to this camp. "Please offer her this." I brought a small leather bag filled with sage out of my coat. "And this." Finally a bag of loose tobacco. "And this, in the way of saying hello."

Sain Tsetseg nodded and made a low sound: hmmmmm. She regarded the gifts slowly, examining each one, nodding her head up and down. Still without saying anything, she turned sideways and carefully reached for a carving of a fish on the end of a strip of leather and offered it. It was a salmon, beautifully etched in gorgeous detail on a reindeer antler. Then the shaman picked up a bag of antelope skin, and offered a handful of crushed flowers. Her hands were thick and blistered, witness to a life of hard work. Although she was a small, sturdy woman, the shaman had a powerful presence, and was very present in her body. A long black braid hung over her shoulder like a rope that held stories.

As we exchanged gifts, we simply looked at one another. Across time. Across continents. Over space. Through eons. Generations passing. Silence. Women had been sitting like this forever. Before time. Before body. We sat. The smells surrounded us, and held us in some other world, out of time. Light wove us together through time and space. I felt at home.

Then came her soft words.

Zaya spoke, "She says she can feel your heart. She is happy you are here. Later she says, perhaps you can exchange readings."

"I would be honored," I replied. "Please ask her if she likes chocolate."

A broad smile transformed the shaman's features into childish glee, her eyes opening wide to reveal both depth and light.

"Please tell her she is welcome in our Tipi Hotel any time, and also that my partner is in there, and that he would be happy to meet her. Please tell her to bring anyone she likes."

Sain Tsetseg listened and nodded. Zaya gestured towards the door, and we opened the flap to be greeted by a bright sun and busy camp life.

I walked to the stream, and began wandering upstream. Something in my soul had slipped into place, an essential part. I had the sense if I died today it would be fine. Complete. Not that I wanted to die, but it was such a feeling of wholeness, like a circle closing, one that I had drawn as a child, but not complete till now, like a gear slipping into place, a sentence dotted with a full stop, an exhale of an inhale begun many years ago.

Later Sain Tsetseg and I had several visits, mostly communicating through gesture, with no translator present. How we journeyed, our drums. Our robes. Our herbs. The heart of a shaman. The death of Sain Tsetseg's son. How she became a shaman. How she loved her daughter and was teaching her. We giggled over chocolate and Russian jam on bread. We sang. Sain Tsetseg tried to teach me words in Tuvan, her language. We hummed. We shared. One morning, Sain Tsetseg entered the Tipi Hotel with two elderly women of the tribe, indicating that one of them needed a massage. This woman looked to be in her late 80s, although she was only 65 years old. There was no one to care for her teeth, and many were missing. She had been injured while riding a reindeer years ago, and her leg was set at an odd angle. Her back was bent with ice and age.

As the woman slowly made her way onto the pad to lie down, Zaya came into the tipi to watch. The woman welcomed the massage I gave her with sounds of contentment. Sain Tsetseg mumbled softly to her friend. The woman said something. Zaya translated, "She says she can feel the snow melting in her side." Silence. A bit later, "She says her eyes are clearing." The woman began to snore, and Sain Tsetseg laughed lightly, giving a sign that meant Good! Everyone sat quietly, listening to the breathing of the elderly one, the sounds of the reindeer outside, and horses munching on grasses nearby.

THE READING

Sain Tsetseg and I sat in her tipi one hot afternoon, the front flap open, slight breezes penetrating the air thick with odors of reindeer and dust. She had indicated it was a good time for a visit, her daughter busy outside collecting flowers that would be used for medicine. Even on a sunny afternoon, the inside of a tipi was fairly dark. Sain Tsetseg sat on the bench near her stove, wearing a loose fitting western dress over pajama bottoms, obviously garb left behind by tourists.

We had agreed to do Readings for one another. We had an interpreter present. I had already read for Sain Tsetseg, and now she was going to read for me. She took out her mouth harp and began playing it. Every now and then she glanced up at me as she played. The sounds seemed to come from a distant place, and felt as though they were coming through her, not created by her.

She played for what seemed like a long time. I closed my eyes and let the sounds take me. Swirling energy filled the tipi, as though a Sufi dancer was twirling round and round. I felt very grounded, not in the swirl, but observing it.

When Sain Tsetseg was finished, the sudden silence jolted me back to my seat on the cushion. I opened my eyes, and looked at this woman. She had both a fierceness and a sweetness about her. "Nobody's fool," I thought. Her persona shifted constantly from shy small woman to focused shaman with a warrior's heart.

After a long silence filled with the buzzing of flies that came and went, and a quick curious peek into the tipi by a reindeer, she began to speak.

"You have powerful guides. Especially the animal. The Ceremony you are being shown is one you need to offer in your land. The Singing one. I see that you sometimes feel very tired of this life. No matter. You are a shaman. That's it. Tired or not, no matter. We have to do our work, and your work is far from done. There are many people who need you, and this ceremony.

"You have so much help. You know this, but sometimes you forget. Don't forget. When you have this feeling of tired, you have to wash yourself with flowers, three days in a row. I will give you the flowers here to use, but you have to find the ones to use where you live.

"I feel your heart beat. It's a good heart. Spend more time with your guides because they are very strong."

She was quiet. She smiled. She said, "And the last thing, don't forget to have fun."

She slowly pulled out a piece of cloth from behind her, and reached in a bag that had once held vegetables. Into the cloth, she placed three handfuls of dried flowers, yellow, red, and rust colored.

She handed me the cloth and indicated I should smell them. The odor was sweet and earthy. "Wash all over using a part of them, for three days. In the morning. Early."

I thanked her, folded the cloth carefully, and stepped out into the hot sun, where the herd of reindeer were circling to keep the flies away.

VISITORS

A man and his wife had traveled from Washington to visit the Reindeer People while we were living there. They had come a long way, and wanted a ceremony from Sain Tsetseg. He was studying to be a shaman, and wanted to videotape her doing a ceremony.

Zaya came into our teepee late one afternoon to explain this to us. We had seen the couple arrive, set up a tent, and immediately go to Sain Tsetseg's tipi. Here was evidence of a problem that the Reindeer People, particularly the shamans, faced.

Tradition said one always asks for permission to see the shaman. And shamans know when someone is coming, even from far away. One evening a pregnant woman, her husband, and son arrived on horseback to seek help from Sain Tsetseg and she had been standing outside her tipi awaiting them. The woman was eight months pregnant, a younger shaman herself, and was seeking help because of problems with her pregnancy. No one had sent word they were coming. Sain Tsetseg just knew.

However, the man and woman from the States, unaware of protocol, marched right over to her tipi upon arriving.

The shamans of the Reindeer People are facing extinction. In fact, the tribe itself is down to a mere 300 or so. Word is out, and people like this man arrive and expect the shamans to perform for them. And the shamans do not know how to say "No." This trait, not directly saying "no" is found also among the Mongolians in the city.

So, Sain Tsetseg did what many of the shaman were resorting to doing. She prepared a fake ceremony to please the man and receive the gifts he had brought. She was not immune to liking sparkly, fancy bracelets or money.

Zaya came in to explain that the shaman was going to put on a fake Ceremony for the man that evening, and that her husband was going to play the part of the shaman's assistant. The drum that would be used was not her real drum. Nothing about the Ceremony would be real. Not the singing, the drumming, the calling to the spirits; all would be a show.

During the night, Wil and I heard the drumming, and it was indeed a beat we had not heard before. Zaya came into our tipi the next morning and told us gleefully how the fake ceremony had gone. Moments later Sain Tsetseg entered, and happily showed us a beautiful silver bracelet with turquoise carving in it. She smiled broadly and left.

When I had read for Sain Tsetseg this very subject had come up. I had seen in her long braid, all her ancestors, and the first women shamans. They were unsettled and arguing amongst themselves. Sain Tsetseg had told me this was what currently happened among the shamans. Some of them traveled to Lake Khövsgöl Nuur to offer fake ceremonies to tourists; others felt this was wrong and were upset by it. Within the tribe there was argument as to how to deal with the tourists.

They had compromised much in the same way some of the Lakota people had done, and in the manner of certain tribes around Santa Fe. Likenesses of real ceremonies and jewelry were crafted to sell to tourists, while the real knowledge was hidden.

I could not judge what I saw. Surely I felt disappointed, but then I had to face the fact that I too had come to meet her. Yes, I was respecting the traditions as best as I knew how, but Wil and I both knew very well that one reason we were welcomed for a month was that we had agreed to purchase many carvings and sell them in the States.

I took comfort in the moments, silent and without interpreter, when Sain Tsetseg came to teach me words from her language, or we sat giggling over a jar of Russian jam and bread. Simple moments of being two women who shared a common legacy over time and distance.

On our last day, I promised to send Sain Tsetseg a truly warm coat. We talked about what was happening with the shamans of the tribe. How Sain Tsetseg was passing her knowledge to her daughter. How one of their most powerful shamans was dying after doing a ceremony for an autistic child on a day when he should not have done it. How the father of the child had profited from the book he wrote about his journey.

Several years ago, the Tsataan—Reindeer People—had been introduced to the Western world through a well meaning Non-Governmental Organization, and I felt strongly that the tribe was near its end. Although well-intentioned, such disruption of a nomadic people with no overarching plan led to chaos. Bits of plastic from well-meaning tourists littered the landscape. Antibiotics had been randomly left behind for them to take. The children often came into the tipi to beg for candy, a learned behavior from the tourists.

Many of the Tsataan now spent the winter in a small town, weakening the link of the tribe. A shaman was dying as a result of offering Ceremonies on days when his Spirits were not in agreement. I felt that Wil and I were witnessing the last of the tribe.

Before leaving, we promised to return and buy many carvings, take them to the States, sell them, and give the tribe the money. We agreed to return in a year, and live with the Reindeer People for a month, bring material for a tipi which we would leave for the tribe.

A DAY IN MONGOLIA

I sat on my sleeping bag in our small tipi, my hand under myself, trying desperately not to pee. This was happening a lot: drinking water and staying hydrated came at the cost of sudden strong urges to pee, a problem because I had to get out of the tipi, and far enough away to crouch behind a bush, and I couldn't run out while holding onto myself.

So I sat there and breathed in, and held my breath, and rocked and hoped the urge would go away. Usually I got about a 30 second break, and in that time, I dashed out, ran along the path I had made behind our tipi to my favorite spot, lifted my skirt, yanked my pants down, and did the deed while the reindeer came running at me, smelling salt.

I knew that everyone in the tribe knew exactly where I was, but this was true of anyone going out to relieve themselves, and was just part of life among the Reindeer People. As was the constant need to fetch and boil water, haul wood, keep the fire going.

Living in a tipi with Wil—who is nearly six feet tall and a man of some stature—was not something I would have thought to be possible, but within a couple of days, we had developed silent agreements about who moved when, who did what, and we managed well.

Taking a bath was another matter. First, the water had to be boiled, and then poured into a round tub about the size of a laundry basket. Then one of us had to stand guard outside, as the traditional placing of a piece of wood across the tipi flap to signal that one was bathing did not impress the dogs. The dogs thought maybe it meant, "Time to eat wooden stick." I stood outside and tried to imagine Wil actually fitting himself into that tub, and resisted the urge to fling the flap open to see. I heard noises like "ahhh" and and "oh yeah" for about five minutes before I could hear him say "enough." A minute later he emerged, somewhat clean in somewhat clean clothing and looking very pleased with himself.

"It's amazing how good warm water feels," he said. "I think I'll take a little walk."

Then there was the aftermath of the bath. The water in the tub was black with dirt. Cleaning up splashed water in the tent. Carrying the tub and dumping the dirty water. Hanging the towel, putting the dirty clothing in a bag for laundry another day. Cleaning out the tub, as it would be used by someone else in the tribe, perhaps later that day. We did this for one another, so that the person who had bathed could actually relax after.

Being clean, as we in the West know clean, simply was not possible. We lived in dirt, were surrounded by reindeer poop, and our clothing was black with dirt when we rinsed it out. We came to accept that as part of daily life, and did our best to brush our teeth and continue basic hygiene.

I had an extra challenge: I had a temporary thing in my mouth that acted as three of my front teeth. I had to wear it till I could get implants, and it had to be kept clean. Every night, I carefully removed it, and washed it, and put it away in its little case. I would not talk to Wil after this, as my vanity would not allow him to see me toothless. I had seen myself in the mirror, and was convinced no amount of love could overcome that gap in my mouth.

I don't know how I managed to keep track of that little mouth piece the whole four weeks, as our small tipi was filled with bags of food, firewood, and clothing, and I was constantly sweeping, moving things around, trying to maintain space for visitors who popped in regularly.

Custom required offering tea and treats to anyone who came to visit, which meant having water on hand and a fire going, and a space for them to sit while waiting.

Custom also dictated that anyone could come in at any moment, without warning, and sit down to visit at any time of day. Not only that, but any family's Spirit Reindeer could also come in, and indeed, had a right to enter. Every family had a Spirit Reindeer, appointed by a shaman, and this animal lived as a member of the family.

One in particular loved to visit our tipi, usually around dinner time, and he had quite the pair of antlers. He would stick his head in first, and soon followed with his large body and wide nose, usually heading straight for the dinner pan.

"NO!" I would shout and wave at him, to no effect. On his own, he usually turned and left when he realized that he was not going to get fed, but on his time, not mine. I suppose that my shouting at him was a bit ill-mannered, but I was not giving away any of our hard-won food to a reindeer who had the whole taiga to munch on!

Cooking was arduous and seemingly never-ending and resulted in the same meal day after day: rice, chopped carrots, onions, and a curry spice. Now and then bread would accompany a meal if we had time to make it.

We had brought protein bars, protein shakes, and protein snacks from the States, and these literally saved our lives. Still, we ran completely out of food once, and twice we nearly ran out. People in the tribe happened to be taking the eight-hour horse ride into town, and graciously brought us rice and vegetables from the one store, but not before we had gone a couple of days without food. Not that any of the tribe considered that to be a big deal: in winter, they often went for weeks without food other than bread and reindeer milk, and thought nothing of it.

Chocolate was my savior. I knew that no matter what happened, at night, every night, I had one square of chocolate to look forward to right before sleep, and I guarded that chocolate like my life. No one other than Wil knew about it, and he had his own supply, and we both knew not to ask the other. Some things are not for sharing.

However, one night, a confluence of events took place. I was sitting on my sleeping bag, back turned to both the tipi entrance and Wil, when the Spirit Reindeer entered and startled me, causing me to drop my three front teeth somewhere on the tipi floor, which was basically dirt. As I desperately began searching for my teeth, Wil asked "What's wrong?" and I murmured something along the lines of "Get that friggin reindeer outta here!" when I suddenly realized I had tipped over my bag of chocolate in my search.

Now I was without teeth and potentially without chocolate and this sent me over the edge. I started shouting (with no front teeth) "Goddamith, wherths my chocolate and my theeth?" Then I started crying. I couldn't see clearly through my tears, and Wil couldn't understand a word I was saying.

He did get the reindeer out, though, and I suddenly found my teeth, which calmed me right down. I cleaned them and, when I placed them in their little container, I came upon my chocolate and realized only one piece had spilled. I was about to toss that outside the tipi when I remembered that it's poison for dogs. I didn't know if that was also true for reindeer but I wasn't about to be responsible for the death of a reindeer, spirit or otherwise.

Calmer now, I got myself together for sleep. Wil was reading, but he looked my way and casually asked, "Everything okay now?"

"Uh hmm." I answered, closed mouthed. "Uh hmmm."

GOODBYE

As Wil and I packed our tipi and readied for leaving the Tsataan, I had very mixed feelings. No part of me wanted to stay. It wasn't anything sentimental. No, I had mixed feelings about the tribe itself. I had never experienced a people so distant, seemingly unfriendly, and without joy. With the exception of Sein Tsetseg, Zaya, TJ, and one other man, no one had been the least bit friendly or even cordial with us during our one month stay. That is, not after the second night when we purchased a large amount of carvings from them. They were plenty friendly the first two days.

I could see that to them, we were just two more outsiders who might be a source of money. And I understood that the cultural separations were probably beyond anything I could imagine. Still, I had stayed among indigenous peoples before, and never had such an experience. It is not that anyone was rude, just totally uninterested and distant. The only time anyone came into our tipi was when they wanted something to eat or drink. Sometimes for a massage, after which they would get up and leave quickly. I was really puzzled by this lack of connection.

I had asked Zaya about it, if Wil and I had done something to offend them. "Oh no," she assured us. I have lived with them for four years as the wife of TJ and they treat me the same way."

To this day I don't understand this and have accepted that I never will. I can make up a million stories in my mind, but that is exactly what they are.....stories. But in all my considerable travels to many countries on this planet, this was the only time I was unable to connect with a people.

Except Sain Tsetseg. She came out to see us off. The others had come into the tipi to see what we might be leaving behind, and indeed we gave away many things, boots, towels, extra food. Each person grabbed what they were offered and hurriedly went running off to their tipi to claim it as their own.

As Wil and I mounted our horses for the ride back up the mountain, I paused and looked at Sain Tsetseg. "I see your heart," I signaled with my hands. Sain Tsetseg nodded in agreement. She signaled, "I see your heart."

LIFE LESSONS FROM THE TSATAAN

When I finally came to Mongolia, after years of longing for it, I found at last a relationship in size between people and land that made sense to my soul: the ratio between the vastness of the steppes and the few people felt very right to me. There are so many of us in the Western world, and I wonder if this isn't the crux of many of our issues: overcrowding. Noise. The stress of living cheek-by-jowl in non-natural spaces.

The two weeks we spent living with a family of Mongolian herders, prior to visiting the Reindeer People felt, in many ways, like the quintessential "right" life to me. Seeing a two year old toddle out of a ger, a yurt-like structure, onto the land, among a herd of goats, with the back of the pants ripped so the child can squat to pee or poo, seemed to represent a kind of natural freedom that we, as a species are losing. The joy of playing with an 11 year old on the hillside, where a simple stick was the only toy we needed, to tumble around on the ground in a game of hide and seek where there is no place to hide, felt so joyful and spontaneous. To fall asleep to the sounds of goats munching in a circle around the ger, and to catch the snakelike eye of a curious goat as he briefly poked his head through the opening was somehow deeply restful. I responded instinctively because, deep in my bones, I remembered a time when our own ancestors lived like this.

Herders in Mongolia live with life-threatening danger every day and, to their credit, it has made them wonderfully cooperative, working together for the survival of all, in direct contrast to the sometimes ruthless competitiveness that often marks Western culture. For instance, the nomads have to be aware of the water sources in a certain range, say 200 miles. Only enough families will set down their gers within that range so that all will have water. Families that own herds of horses will share that land of no fences with families that herd goats and sheep, as these animals require different grasses, so everyone will be able to eat. No matter who shows up on horseback at what hour, a bowl of fermented milk will be offered, and although it may be a two-hour horseback ride home to the ger, a fire will be lit and someone in the family will make sure to offer help upon arrival.

And yet life there was difficult and even cruel and, ultimately, I could not sustain it. My back could not sustain the endless gathering of dung for the fire. I could not yank back the head of a sheep to cut its throat and then butcher and cook it. Nor could I stand the below-freezing winter temperatures, and the misery of watching a horse freeze to death in the unforgiving winds that swept the landscape.

But again, there were times when I sat on a hillside, and another nomadic herder would walk up out of nowhere, as part of his daylong journey with his cattle, or yak, and sit beside me and smile as though it was perfectly natural to find a white woman out in the middle of Mongolia. He would sit and point to the grass and begin teaching me his language as if he was my appointed language professor. These times stay in my heart: that a complete stranger from across the world would roll over in laughter at my mispronunciation of a word and slap me on the back in glee. These encounters give me hope for humanity.

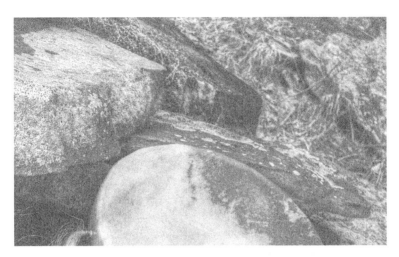

— PART IV —

SINGING INTO BONE

Twenty five years ago, I received a tattoo of a morpho butterfly on my upper chest. Butterflies had accompanied me my whole life, sometimes appearing in the least likely of places—as in the visitation during the storm on the Costa Rican mountainside. Both fragile and strong, butterflies know their migration routes, and withstand all manner of weather. Like them, my transformation has involved riding the waves of change in location, always following the call of Spirit, even when that looked untenable to others. Now I have come to rest, not to end life, as butterflies do, but to land and deepen.

Here is a taste of what my life is now, now that I rest easily and have a secure boundary in which to stretch my wings. I wandered the world, first as a lost young woman trying to find her inner compass and, later, accompanied by my magical tools and a few soul-companions, as a healer called to many corners of this beautiful earth. And in the end, although I still travel, I have found my true home, reached my true center, gone deep to the beautiful bones of my life.

MY DRUM

I have several drums, but my favorite is one I have had for about 15 years now. It was for sale in a shop near Seattle, and I noticed it as soon as I entered the store, thinking, "That's my drum." I asked to play it, and after I learned its history, who made it, and how the materials were gathered, I purchased it.

It is an elk drum, with long strands of horse hair hanging from it. This is the drum I have traveled with to many countries, and it feels like a best friend. It is one of the few objects I own that I want to be burned with me when I die, along with my soul bundle and robe and hat.

My drum is a heart beat. Not only my heart beat, but the heart beat of the planet. When I hold the drum, my left hand fits through the back cross of it and finds a comfortable old resting place. I know that different places on the hide create different tones, and I know these tones like knowing the voice of an old friend.

I use this drum when I am doing a ceremony, particularly Singing into Bone, which is a Ceremony where I sing people down into the wisdom of their bones. This Ceremony was given to me while I visited the Reindeer People, and is all about sounds entering the body and shifting the flow of energy through the bones to help people remember who they are and what they came for.

Usually there are four other drummers for this Ceremony, one in each direction, but it is my drum that allows me to sing because other voices come through it. I never begin singing till I hear these voices and I don't experience myself as singing alone during it. The voices enter through the drum, and they are as clear as any chorus. Also the sounds that the people carry within them come to me through my drum, through a part of the hide that is marked like a quarter moon, and these sounds help me know what to sing back to the people.

My drum can gallop like a horse, traveling far up into the heavens to create a place for the people to fall through to enter their bones. It is like creating a shaft of light down into the earth and meeting everyone there in the form of skeletons, and my drum leads the way.

When I teach classes, my drum usually has its own seat next to me, or near me. It is rare, but at times I have let someone play my drum, usually people who have no sense of their own power at all. Within two minutes of playing my drum they are transformed and stand in wonder at the possibility of expressing their own power.

The horse hair on my drum likes to be combed and cared for, groomed like a horse. The hair likes to be wrapped in a circle and tucked in the back, and when I do this, I feel like I am combing my daughter's hair. My drum loves its case, made by Nina Maluda, who also made my shaman's robe. Nina is a spirit sister who lives in Seattle and worked as my assistant for many years. She made the case for my drum, and it's the only case this drum wants to be in; I have tried putting it in other cases, and I can sense it is not happy.

My drum has a life of its own. On a physical level, of course it needs to be warm to sound its best. But there is something else entirely that happens with my drum. If the spirit of an occasion is off somehow, meaning the timing is off, or someone in the room is not totally present, my drum simply will sound flat no matter how warm it is. This is a signal to me to share something about how I am teaching, or address something about the energy in the room. My drum never lies.

I have seen my drum hanging in my healing room, seen the light of the sun shine through it while placing it carefully on a hook in a gazebo at Pura Vida Retreat Center in Costa Rica, looked through its elk hide to watch the clouds come and go while doing Ceremony on land. I have seen my drum sit contentedly listening to the lessons of the medicine wheel. My drum has lulled people into caves to meet their spirit helpers, deep into the earth, up into the sky, has led them on pathways through the forest and along the sea. As long as I have a heartbeat, my drum will sound.

LISTENING
IN THE BELLY

Patricia had a huge belly. She sometimes talked with me about the big belly healers, about how energy is transformed within the belly, at the point a couple of inches below the navel which is a powerful center of energy.

She taught me to listen in my belly. Rather than listening with my mind—up in my head—to the stories of others, I learned to put my energy and attention in my abdomen and feet. When I hear very emotional stories, and stay in my belly, I can be present without getting caught up in the drama of the story. Another way Patricia said this was "to stay in the balcony with my popcorn," meaning that we need to develop the ability to observe feelings and thoughts without reacting to them. Being in the belly allows me to hear the tone and tenor of a story, not the drama.

I learned to get in my belly by first connecting to my feet touching the bare earth, a practice that extended to being barefoot in the snow, on rough trails, on the sands of beaches, in the rainforest, on rocky paths, till my feet were tough but fully connected with the earth's energy, and I could run that energy through my body.

Then I focused on my breath, not changing it, just being aware of it, particularly in my belly. Next came an awareness of the physical sensation of my heartbeat. This practice too became so normal to me that awareness of my heartbeat became part of my daily experience of my body. And finally, I focused on awareness of the air around me. However, the center of all this was in my belly.

At one time, I used to offer Energetic Readings at a bookstore in Portland, Oregon. I did this by sitting opposite the person and first asking permission to see and feel her energy field, and then placing my hands about eight inches from her, and scanning her body. In this way, I received her story, her ancestral background, and images of her soul path.

Usually after doing this, people would sit and listen to what I had to say, or to the information that came through. Then we would have a conversation, my part always coming from listening in my belly. This one woman, however, started talking immediately, not giving me a second to say anything after reading her energy.

I sat back and listened from my belly, tuning into her gestures, rhythms, the frantic quality of her movements and tone. She talked quickly and strung her sentences together in a way that allowed her to breathe but not stop talking. She continued telling me the story of her ex-husband and his abusive behavior, their very dramatic divorce which had become public as she was well known in the area, and the stories of losing custody of her children and the media talking about her in an untrue way. She talked on and on till we had only five minutes left for the Reading.

My belly felt calm, but as I listened, I began to see an energy around her, pounding on her, rather like a circle of rattles that kept her so wound up in her story that she could not escape it even for a moment. It was as though the bottom of a stream bed had been stirred up and could not settle. She did not want a reading. She wanted to tell and retell her story.

With five minutes left, she suddenly got quiet.

"So, what did you see?" she asked me.

"I saw a woman stuck in her story," I replied.

"You saw WHAT?" she asked, offended.

"I saw you sit here and talk for 55 minutes, repeating your story. Not asking me till now what I saw."

"I talked for 55 minutes! Why didn't you stop me? You are supposed to give me a Reading! I paid you for a Reading."

"Well, in order to do that, I have to have time to speak. I tried to interrupt you a couple of times, but you kept talking, so I listened. I heard your story, and what I saw was that you need to step out of your story, out of the energy of it. "

"Well, how am I supposed to do that?"

"I think you need to—pardon the expression—go jump in the lake! I would suggest you go to the nearest stream that you can get into stark naked, and lie there in it as long as you can stand it. Maybe go with someone who can be like a guard for you, so you don't have to worry about other people. Just stay in there as long as possible. When you come out, have very warm clothing to put on, and sit in the sun. "

"And this will do what?"

"It will stop your story in its tracks."

She stood up, perturbed, and I gave her the tape I had recorded.

"Then, "I said, "When you get home, listen to this, every word, without interruption. Listen to the tone of your voice, the feelings. When you are done listening, label this as My Tape Number 11. Or whatever number you want. Whenever you start this story up in your mind again, say to yourself, 'Oh, that's Tape Number 11.'"

"That's your advice to me?" she asked at the doorway.

"That's it," I said. "Here is my email. Feel free to contact me after you have done what I suggested."

She left, upset and no doubt on her way to complain that the shaman upstairs was a very poor Reader.

Much to my surprise, however, she did not complain. Instead, I received an email from her a month later. She stated that, at her wit's end, she had taken my advice and jumped in a stream and, much to her amazement, found great relief in the cold of the water, and was able to stay in it for quite awhile. She had been going back three times a week. This had become her "safe place" and for the first time since her decision to ask for a divorce, which had been a couple of years ago, she was sleeping and able to think clearly. Whenever she began the story in her mind, she said "That's Tape

11," and her mind cleared. She told me she thought she would be ready to listen to what I had to say in about two more weeks, and would return for another Reading and thanked me profusely.

KNOW WHERE
YOU SHOULDN'T GO

We nearly collided as we ran to the departure gate, my assistant Nina and I, rushing to catch the flight to Trinidad. I had traveled from Costa Rica, she from Seattle, and both flights arrived late, leaving us to greet each other on the run.

Not till we were seated on the plane, having arrived just as the last passengers were boarding, did we look at each other and laugh.

"We have to quit meeting like this." I said. "Thanks for coming."

"My pleasure," Nina replied in her usual understated fashion.

I had met Nina in Costa Rica, where she was participating in a yoga retreat at Pura Vida. She entered the healing tent for a session, and I noticed both a sweetness and a sense of heaviness in her energy. During the session it became apparent that she wanted her work to reflect more of her spirit. The heaviness also reflected the ongoing care of her mother that Nina had singlehandedly taken on, with little support.

Nina continued to seek me out during breaks after our session. This was unusual, since most clients left me alone, but Nina was polite yet persistent in her repeated attempts to converse with me, rather like a bird that keeps calling till its tone takes on a meaning. I came out of my somewhat protective haze to realize a connection was in the making.

The following year, I visited Nina in her home in Seattle where she organized sessions for me, and she indicated that she was interested in learning what I could teach about energetic healing. I began instructing her, and found over the next two years that she had unique and hard-to-find abilities, including the skill to ground me when I was journeying and act as an energy center for me to find my way home, rather like a beacon on a runway. Many shamans' assistants are trained in this skill; I had never met anyone who possessed the quality as if they had been born to it. Nina became my assistant in Ceremony and in sessions that required me to journey to the Spirit World. Nina's eyes always sparkled, and she had the sturdy frame of a grounded woman, a rare find in this world. Her presence was a huge benefit to me and others.

Over the next few years, Nina grew more and more adept at seeing energy shifts and feeling the energies present, and her training in Qi Gong and Tai Chi added to her awareness.

However, Nina's abilities extended into the creative realm, too. She was a sewer and maker of amazing magical, spiritual objects, and a clever designer: she gutted the insides of a piece of luggage and converted it into a traveling case for all my crystals, rocks, and healing materials, crafted a gorgeous case for my drum, and eventually created my shaman's robe and hat.

But the quality that Nina always had, no matter where we were or what we did, was an ability to be very kind to people. And sweet. She was a great balance to my "let's get to it" approach in working with people. A gentle energy to hold them, an assuring voice to comfort them, a welcoming presence to greet them.

Now she had agreed to come to Trinidad with me to assist with a series of sessions I was offering, as well as to be present at meetings with an alternative doctor and a group of women.

We were staying as guests in the home of a wealthy couple who had access to many people of all socio-economic backgrounds. They had graciously offered me a separate healing space and apartment, and a room in their home for Nina. The home was gated. In fact, we were met at the airport by an armed bodyguard, who was to shadow us whenever we traveled outside the grounds of the house. As we headed from the airport to our destination, we asked why we needed to be guarded and he mentioned something about kidnappings and murders. He was quite serious.

My clients in Trinidad ranged from women who had been brutally abused to a man who had been severely beaten the night before because he was contesting the current government. There was an air of violence surrounding nearly every session, and Nina and I soon abandoned any ideas we had about a peaceful, beautiful Caribbean island experience.

After a week of challenging sessions, we took off (or rather were driven off, our bodyguard with us) to what was to be a vacation spot by the beach for a couple of days. Left there on our own, we breathed a shared sigh of relief to be near the gracious, gorgeous ocean, and to have some relaxation. Nina spent the night on the beach, accompanied by two giant turtles who came to shore, sat near her, and then swam out to sea as the sun rose. I slept, but was irritated by shadowy forms in my dreams that kept me from resting deeply.

In the morning, we were sitting at the outdoor breakfast table by the ocean when a man appeared about 30 yards in front of us on the beach, screaming at his wife and brandishing a machete. She defended herself with a shovel, the two of them like lions locked in battle. Glass from a broken bottle that he tossed at her landed in our eggs, and as we stood to get under cover, we heard the clanging of the shovel against the machete. His screams and hers alerted the townspeople who were now also yelling and shouting, followed by the sirens of a police car. Nina and I slowly retreated into our hotel room, and made plans to leave and have breakfast--without glass--somewhere else.

Later, escaping to a beautiful rainforest resort, I stood on the

Welcome Center's balcony talking with a man who revealed that he was a New York Times reporter covering a story on a recent kidnapping, which had resulted in several chopped-up bodies in the forest. It seemed violence followed us on this trip no matter where we went.

Still later, we visited the home of an alternative doctor who had coordinated sessions for a number of women. By the end of the day it was clear to Nina and me that these women needed a support group of their own. I suggested such a group, and was met by silence. One of the women later told me they would love to form a group, but did not know how it would be possible without the permission of their husbands. I suggested to her that they simply tell their husbands they were going to make clothing together, or do some craft activity. I was hopeful, but when I saw the fear in her eyes, I knew that perhaps forming a group would be too difficult.

We were taken to see an artists' co-op, and as I entered the room of a famous artist, suddenly I could barely breathe and I began shaking and feeling unsteady. Nina helped me out to the hallway, where I began to see flashes of light in the corner of my right eye. The energy in the artists' room was so filled with blackness, darkness, and death that I could not gain my feet. We waited until I could walk to leave.

On the way to the airport, again with the bodyguard, Nina and I were a bit numb. Not that we hadn't seen many beautiful qualities in Trinidad: sessions had been powerful and satisfying, the mix of cultures was fascinating, there was a lot of lively, life-filled music, and artists in abundance. But the one word that encapsulated the experience was 'violence.'

It wasn't till a year later, after a Ceremony done by a Siberian shaman in Seattle, that my eye returned to normal. That shaman said one important thing to me after journeying on my behalf..."There are places on this earth you should not go. You have to get smart enough to know where those places are. You are not Mother Teresa." Excellent advice.

HEALING SESSIONS

My healing room is upstairs in the house my husband Wil and I recently bought outside of Woodstock, NY. After a round of four seasons plus one on this land, I have begun to feel at home, knowing when certain birds will alight on what branches, the hidey holes of chipmunks and woodchucks and the likely turf of voles. Having seen a couple of black bears pad their silvery way across the property, heard the mating calls of the owls, and located the prime spots for web building, I have begun to find my place within the scheme of things here.

The seasons are my markers and living in a four season

climate is such a holding, akin to the feeling in Costa Rica of being held by the land. Only here, I feel held by the seasons, and all the rhythmic cues that accompany them.

My healing room is a large space, with windows that open onto the forest, the artesian pond, and the front gardening spaces. It doubles as my art room, and the grey floor is speckled with paint from the previous owner's artwork. The ceiling has blown-in insulation which we had done last winter, and it looks like snow, except for the steel supports that show through every two feet. I have no intentions of making the room any more civilized than it is.

Also in this room are my large healing altar and all my tools. About half the room is for healing, and as well as the massage table covered by a beautiful blanket with a pattern of running horses, there are two chairs for sitting and chatting. This space is all mine. I love it.

We had a giant furnace installed which comes through the healing room in all its silver glory, wraps around one wall, and jets heat out through three blowers. I have a little pad on the floor where I love to rest and stare out at the forest, and the heater's sounds are quite comforting to me, especially when looking out at icicles or snow.

I am standing to the right of my client, a woman lying on her back on the massage table, covered with a cozy blanket. She has 4th stage metastasized breast cancer, which she has had for five years now. When she phoned and inquired about a session, I imagined someone who would look weakened, but when she arrived, her life energy seemed bright and healthy to me, and I wondered what was going on.

When I do a session for someone, I begin about five steps behind them, arms outstretched, and each step I take towards them, I am feeling into the ancestral lineage both on the mother's and father's sides of the family. Each step is a generation. Sometimes I begin further back, depending on the person and what they have come for.

As I step through the generations, I receive definite feelings of struggle, support, big shifts. Sometimes I will see a guardian or a Spirit Guide. I then trace down one side of the client's body, my hands about eight inches from them, not touching them. I receive information. My hands hurt wherever they encounter pain. I have learned over the years to identify many of these pains, as cancer, grief, accidents, falls, certain illnesses depending on where the pain is. I also see scenes from childhood that affected the person, and sometimes hear them as well.

Now I switch to the other side, and receive whatever information that side has to offer. Many times there is a great imbalance between the two sides, or the top half and bottom half. Over the years, there are patterns of energetic blockages that have made themselves known.

I then place my hands above each chakra, again not touching

the person. All this is part of an energetic diagnosis, so I know where to begin with the healing process, and also get a sense of where the roots of any imbalances are.

I sit in silence next to the person, and ask if any other information needs to come through. If I get a sense that there is something important and it isn't coming to me, I tell the client that I am going to drum and ask for more information.

I do this, asking the Grandmothers to show me what needs to be seen. The Grandmothers are a group of indigenous of women who started appearing about 20 years ago. When I drum and sing and ask for them, they come and show me what the person needs in a way that I might not otherwise see.

When all this is complete, I sit by the person on the massage table, and tell them what information I have received, in the most positive, honest, and hopeful way I can.

Then we make an agreement as to how I am going to work with them, and I begin. Or rather we begin, as it is a collaborative process. I do nothing without the client's permission, and without explaining what I am doing and why.

This particular woman had come to me because she was considering stopping the chemo treatments that she had been taking for many years. Her acupuncturist felt the need for such treatments had passed.

Whenever I'm dealing with a physical illness I make it very clear that I am not a doctor, and I have never claimed to be one. That being said, many times an illness is the result of an emotional/energetic blockage, much the way an illness might be seen by an acupuncturist. One big difference is that some illnesses involve the soul, and this might require a ceremony. Many healing sessions do not require that I journey, only that I see clearly and begin to shift the energetic flow within the person's body.

As I scanned this client's body, what fascinated me was that I had none of the feeling in my hands that I receive when someone has cancer. Absolutely none.

I mentioned this to her. She replied that three healers had told her she no longer had cancer.

I choose to err on the conservative side, so I took another look, specifically at her liver. There was a sense there of being very newly healed. I also began to feel the tiredness in her body from the chemo, though she had more capacity for it than many.

I did not go into her family history with her, as I felt she was current. By that I mean she was not in reaction to childhood triggers, and indeed, she seemed very present to me. Instead of the usual treatment, I asked her to sit back up and talk with me.

As she sat, we looked at one another and burst out laughing at the same time. I said, "I don't think you need a treatment really."

She said, "I know, right?"

I said, "This isn't your story."

She said, "Yes! All these people come up to me and wonder how I am still alive. People who know my story or have heard of it, and all the operations, come up and just burst out crying. The thing is, all these years, I HAVE NEVER BOUGHT INTO THIS CANCER STORY. That is exactly right. IT'S NOT MY STORY."

I know there are many beliefs about how we bring illness on ourselves, etc. etc. I don't for a moment pretend to know WHY different people get particular diseases, and it is not my job to know. My job is to help them heal, whatever that might look like.

"Not quite time to give up the chemo," I told her.

"That's what I think too," she said.

"Maybe another couple of months."

"Till my liver continues to show no cancer," she said.

"Yep," I said.

"Yep," she said.

We laughed again. End of session.

BY THE POND

I am sitting outside our home, about ten minutes outside of Woodstock, New York, at the foot of the Southern Catskills. On our land is an artesian pond, very beautiful and sweet, surrounded by large rocks and one particularly swirly, strong tree that I think of as The Guardian.

The pond is beautiful. On a sunny day, the tree reflects straight down into the seven feet of water, that is clear and always moving since the source is an artesian spring. I have come to know this pond in all four seasons, but now I am getting to know it at night. I am sitting out at 11pm, having hung one string of lights through the forest—just enough light for me to see if a bear is coming.

As I sit, I look up and notice my old friend, Orion. The Milky Way is clear; the sky is filled with stars. It's one of those nights that reveal the layers of darkness, some stars appearing closer and brighter. Because it is nearly winter, there are fewer bird calls than before, and not yet any owls. Only the sound of the small stream of water flowing into the pond can be heard, and an occasional creak of a tree limb.

As I sit, I realize how much I love the cloak of darkness. What a relief and a release it is, to not have to be in any certain form. I am out here in my pajamas and bathrobe, and I have a cup of tea in my hand. Just sitting. Not expecting anything. Just there.

It is in these moments that I am most grateful for being alive on this earth. In the stillness and silence when my heart can open and I can relax into the moment. I think about how all the spiritual work in the world is useless if it doesn't add up to living more tolerantly on a day to day basis in this world.

Sometimes I am so overcome by the beauty of one leaf or

one insect that I cannot fathom all the life forms on this planet. I cannot quite grasp the enormity of the mystery of it all. Perhaps I am not meant to. I know that I am not meant to understand it, because no matter how much I think I understand, I am in a body, and being in a body limits my view. I know this from journeying.

What I know is how much I will never know. What I know is that there is a perfect balance and harmony in the natural world, one that, in our arrogance, we have messed with irrevocably. And I know that any little space and time that aligns me with the natural world is precious to me.

I have deeply considered the religions of the world. And in each there seem to be nuggets of wisdom. But it has never been my experience that I needed someone to intercede between me and Creator....I have always had direct access and believe anyone can. I have never really understood the need for religions, or the draw of them.

For me, the ants, the birds, and bears, the rhythms of nature have been my teachers. The trees, my shelter. The earth and sky my churches since as far back as I can remember. I never liked going inside to worship anything as a child, and insisted that I not be made to return to temple after age eight.

As I sit outside on this night, I had been longing to hear the barred owl that usually comes with his mate. It is time, but the weather has been unseasonably warm, and...no owls. It makes me sad, as I miss them and have been looking forward to seeing them again.

Contemplating that maybe being in this area is not in their best interests, I am just letting go of this idea when I hear an owl hoot. One owl only. No answer. So I answer in my best hoot possible. Nothing. Long silence, and then I hear it again. Closer. A series of hoots. This is the beloved barred owl. He is close by, but of course I can't see him. I am sure he can see me.

"I am so happy you have come back. I have been waiting for you," I speak into the night. Silence. Then a series of hoots, very close by. I sit there, feeling honored that he would visit. I begin talking for about 20 minutes. Every now and then he hoots in return. I know that when he takes off I will not hear the whoosh of wings, as owls are totally silent in flight.

However, I listen carefully after a long silence, thinking he has gone. Then he hoots, but from farther away, and—much to my delight—there comes an answer. I can't tell if it is another male announcing territory, or the call of his mate, but in my romantic mind, I am hoping it's his mate.

Slowly I get up and make my way back into the house. This encounter leaves me happier than any church service ever could, more in touch with life than most encounters with people, and at peace. I know that some tribes believe owls are the harbingers of death. I have not experienced them in this way, though I have used their feathers to help dying people along their way.

For me owls have always been about the Great Mystery

that is life. The way they turn their heads, their silent flight, their gorgeous forms, the way they hunt, their ability to see. Their presence, otherworldly and magnificent. The training of their young, and the amount of territory they need, according to their species.

Why, I wondered, as I entered the house, was it only humans who seemed so out of sync with the natural world? Who view that world as something to be conquered and used for their means only? Why, when we were the species most capable of acting as stewards of this planet, were we the ones destroying it?

As I was about to close the door to the house, I heard one last call from the owl. I said a silent thank you for the state-owned watershed land behind us that was forever protected, could not be walked on, used for hunting, camping, or as a trail. No humans were welcome on it, and that, I thought, was just as it should be.

SINGING INTO BONE

I am standing in a large space, surrounded by people lying on mats, pillows, whatever they have brought to be comfortable. They have gathered to receive the Ceremony I was given in Mongolia, Singing into Bone. I have been offering this Ceremony for five years now, nationally and internationally.

As I look at the people around me and at each of the four drummers who has come to assist in the Ceremony, I thank Sain Tsetseg for encouraging me to follow my spirit animals and to offer this Ceremony.

In both shamanism and Lakota teachings, sound is extremely important. In fact, at the root, sound and light come before form. In my experience, sound not only comes prior to the manifestation of form, sound can affect change in form. Healing.

I have explained this to the participants as best as I can. They have made an intention for themselves, regarding what information they would like to receive in this ceremony. Our bones are the parts of ourselves that remain, and within the marrow are passages that can be sung into. Within those passages is ancestral wisdom of who we came to be, our next steps, and who or what might guide us.

During this Ceremony, if people follow the sounds and the drums, they will receive information vital to them, and it is my responsibility to both sing them into their bones and then sing them their own sounds, the sounds emanating from their bones, that they may hear themselves and remember.

The altar is set; the people are ready, and the drummers too. I put on my Shaman's robe and hat which offer me protection. I begin drumming and the four drummers join me in a heartbeat rhythm.

I first call out to the four directions, asking—no, begging—with sound…that the gates be opened for this Ceremony and that the Gate Keepers watch over us. When I see that the gates are opened and tended, I begin sending sounds way out into the universe, usually through a hole of light I clearly see that goes up to the stars and beyond. I sing and sing till I find an opening and then I begin, with my voice, to create a passageway down.

I sing us down, down from the heavens through the atmosphere, down down into the earth. The singing goes on and on and I have been joined by many other singers as soon as I begin the passage way down.

The Grandmothers come through singing their eternal song from time to time, a sign that all is well.

Onwards and down we tone, making room for all the bodies, all the bones, till I see everyone lying deep in the earth, only their bones, not their bodies.

I begin listening to the sounds coming from the bones, and I sing them back to the people. I see which people have recently lost someone dear to them, who is ill, who is well, but I ignore all this and keep singing into their bones.

I sing every sound that needs to be sung to cleanse them and allow them to receive the wisdom there in the bones.

When it is done, I begin singing them up again. None of the singing feels that it comes from me, but rather through me from some other source. My job is to stay out of the way and let the sounds come forward.

The chorus joins me as I sing the people back into form, back into body, and back into the room. Back into organs, and blood flow and air and skin. Back to this world, this day, this moment. I call out to the gates to close. I thank the Gate Keepers.

I drum faster and faster, the other drummers with me, till we all stop. Suddenly. Silence. It is done.

Often people lie without moving for a long time, which is as it should be. They slowly come back. They have been sung into their bones.

I ask them not to speak about their experience for at least three days and nights, to give the sounds a chance to wash around in their bodies. To make their wisdom known. I ask the people not to give away their experience in words, at least for three days, but to hold it and let it settle.

People have written to me from many places in the world telling me what they experienced. It is healing. Healing. I thank my teachers. I thank Patricia, and the shaman of Chirripo and I thank Sain Tsetseg.

May these words be of benefit to all creatures.

CPSIA information can be obtained
at www.ICGtesting.com
Printed in the USA
FSOW03n1019290317
32303FS